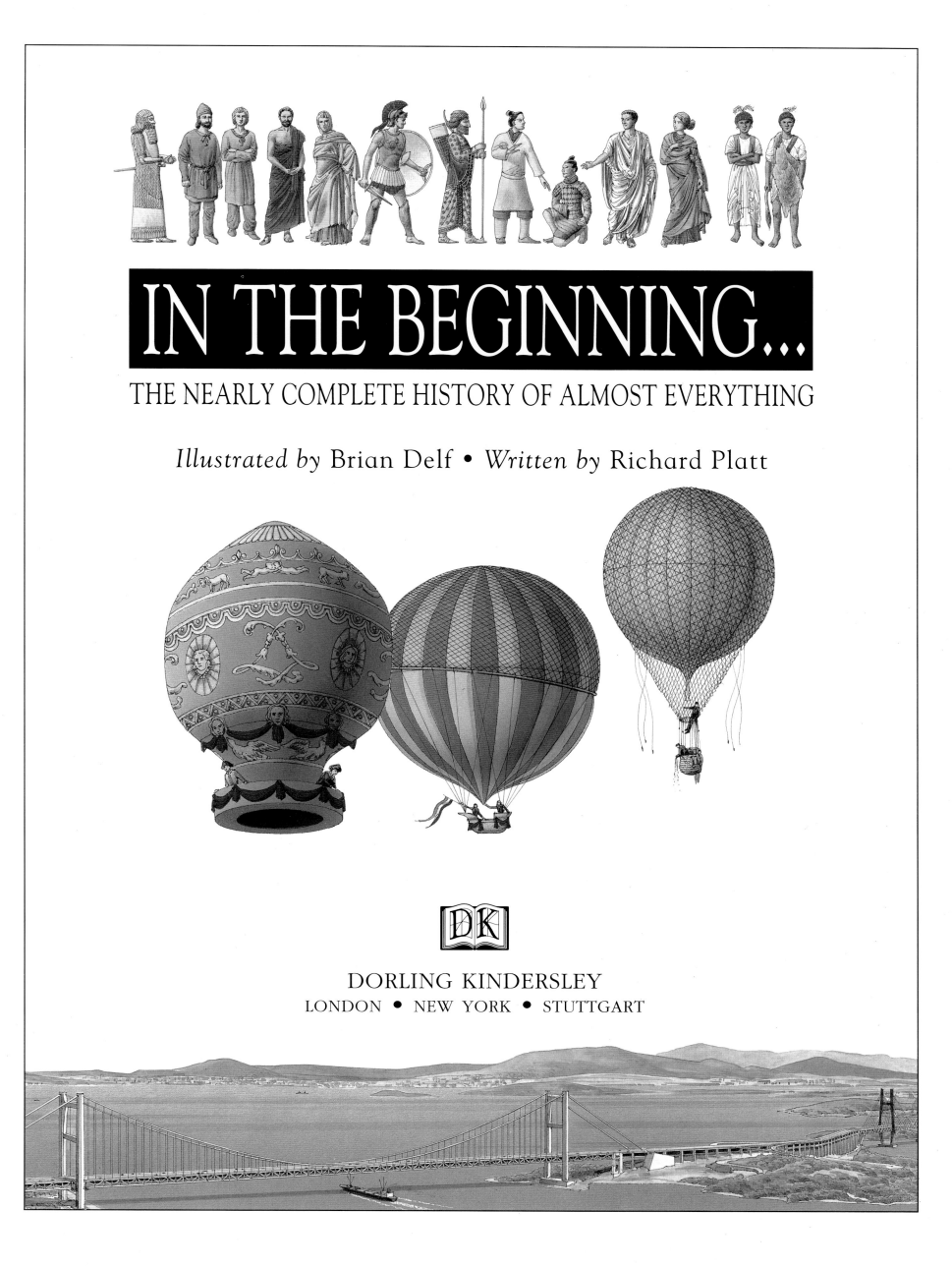

IN THE BEGINNING...

THE NEARLY COMPLETE HISTORY OF ALMOST EVERYTHING

Illustrated by Brian Delf • Written by Richard Platt

DORLING KINDERSLEY

LONDON • NEW YORK • STUTTGART

CONTENTS

A DORLING KINDERSLEY BOOK

Art Editor Dorian Spencer Davies
Designers Sharon Grant, Sara Hill
Senior Art Editor C. David Gillingwater
Project Editor Constance Novis
Senior Editor John C. Miles
U.S. Editor Camela Decaire
Production Louise Barratt
Consultant Eryl Davies

Art Director Roger Priddy

First American edition, 1995
2 4 6 8 10 9 7 5 3 1
Published in the United States
by Dorling Kindersley Publishing, Inc.,
95 Madison Avenue, New York, New York 10016

Copyright © 1995
Dorling Kindersley Limited, London

All rights reserved under International and Pan-American
Copyright Conventions. No part of this publication
may be reproduced, stored in a retrieval system,
or transmitted in any form or by any means,
electronic, mechanical, photocopying, recording
or otherwise, without the prior written
permission of the copyright owner. Published
in Great Britain by Dorling Kindersley Limited.
Distributed by Houghton Mifflin Company, Boston.

Library of Congress Cataloging–in–Publication Data

In the beginning / illustrated by Brian Delf
written by Richard Platt – – 1st American ed.
p. cm. – Includes indexes.
ISBN 0-7894-0206-8
1. Civilization – – History– – Pictorial works – – Juvenile literature.
I. Delf, Brian.
II. Title.
CB69.2.P57 1995
909 – – dc20   95 – 2427
                                   CIP
                                   AC

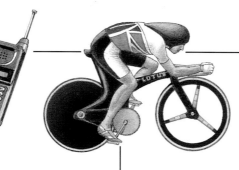

MYSTERY AND MYTH HIDE THE EXACT BEGINNINGS OF ALMOST EVERYTHING. DID A FROG OR A FISH DIVE TO THE BOTTOM OF THE SEAS, SWIMMING UP WITH SOIL TO BUILD THE UNIVERSE? DID THE FIRST MAN AND WOMAN HATCH FROM AN EGG-SHAPED COSMOS? DID AN ALL-POWERFUL GOD CREATE THE HEAVENS AND EARTH? OR DID OUR UNIVERSE BEGIN SOME FIFTEEN BILLION YEARS AGO WITH A TREMENDOUS THERMONUCLEAR EXPLOSION?

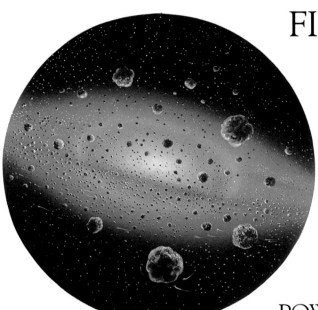

Planets forming from dust and ice

In the next few pages you can see a scientific view of creation: how the cosmos started; how the Earth and other planets formed; and how the first living creatures developed and flourished in the warm, shallow seas of the young world. However, we may never know for sure how the story really began. And as long as there is uncertainty, every culture and religion will tell and retell its own version of the creation story.

Our planet – Earth

Volcanic activity preceded life on Earth

Early human making tools

WE'RE PRETTY SURE THE FIRST HUMANS WERE AFRICAN, BUT WE KNOW LITTLE MORE THAN THAT. Nobody knows who made the first clothes. We have lost the identity of the people who first put spoken words into writing. Who devised the wheel? Or the sailboat? These people, too, have slipped through cracks between history's floorboards. But as we trace the development of the objects that surround us, the picture becomes more focused.

Arab sailing boat

IN THE MORE RECENT PAST WE CAN IDENTIFY WHERE THINGS BEGAN, AND PERHAPS GUESS THE NATIONALITY OF AN INVENTOR OR TWO. Sometimes, as if reading an unfinished detective novel, we come tantalizingly close to the birth of a new idea. Spectacles, for example, were unknown before 1286. An Italian made the first pair in Pisa when the famous leaning tower was only 15 years old. Friar Giordano, a priest in the city, actually spoke to the man who created "little disks for the eyes." But alas, the priest did not recall his name.

"Little disks for the eyes"

MORE RECENTLY STILL, HISTORY RECORDS NAMES AND DATES BUT EVEN THE MOST CLEAR-CUT STORIES TURN OUT TO BE IMPRECISE. For instance, American Samuel Morse generally takes the credit for the electric telegraph. However, 62 people disputed his claim. Further, as technology has become more complex, the role of the individual has shrunk. Modern challenges require more human ingenuity than one individual – or even one nation – can provide. Today's great scientific projects, such as space programs, rely on the participation of thousands of people. Perhaps, in the end, these new enterprises will bring us closer to solving the first great riddle of how it all began.

Samuel Morse

Apollo spacecraft

BIG BANG

**15 billion years ago (bya)
The Big Bang**

The
Universe
explodes
and cools

*As gravity squeezed
denser regions of the
Universe, it set them spinning.
The smaller they shrank, the
faster the spinning became.*

*The outward-throwing force of the
spinning balanced the inward pull
of gravity – creating a stable star.*

*What caused the vast explosion that gave birth to
the Universe? What existed before that moment?
Physics has answers for these difficult questions,
but even some scientists prefer to credit God
with the moment of creation.*

A star is born

*The temperature of the
Universe dropped by half
each time its size doubled.*

*The furnace of the Big Bang created
matter – tiny particles – from energy.*

Creation of the elements

The best explanation that science can
offer about the origin of the Universe is
that it began as a singularity – a minutely small,
hot, dense object. In a vast explosion, this fiery, heavy thing blew
itself apart. The Big Bang created the ingredients that formed the
Universe. This idea was first proposed in the 1920s. Nobody can
prove that it is accurate because there were no people around to
take notes. However most of the evidence that scientists have
collected has supported the Big Bang theory.

After perhaps a hundredth of a second, the Universe
had expanded to the size of our Sun, but much
hotter. It was mostly made of energy, but as it expanded,
matter formed. At first, it was mostly electrons – the
tiniest particles in atoms. A few larger particles formed,
too. There were small numbers of neutrons and protons,
the particles that make up the nucleus (core) of an
atom. Within a couple of minutes, there were nuclei of
hydrogen and helium.

*Inside the newborn
stars, nuclear fusion –
the joining of light
atoms to form heavier
ones – created new
elements.*

The Universe continued to expand and cool,
but a million years or so passed before energy
levels had dropped low enough for electrons,
neutrons, and protons to combine as atoms of
hydrogen and helium. Even today, these two gases
make up 99 percent of all matter. When the atoms
formed, they were drawn together into clouds by
gravity. Squeezed into ever-smaller spaces, the atoms
reacted, and the temperature rose again.

*Our own Sun formed out of
the remains of supernovas that
exploded elsewhere in the Universe*

**5 bya
The Solar
System begins**

These regions of the Universe became stars. Cooked
inside, hydrogen and helium turned into heavier
elements. (The elements are the 90 or so basic types of
matter that combine to make everything.) Spinning in
space, the stars became bigger, hotter, and heavier.

Our Solar System began some 5 billion years ago. It started when dust,
ice, and gas collapsed to create a dense region, a "protostar." Around
this core circled a cloud of more gas and dirty ice. The gravitational pull of
the core region drew some of the matter in, and eventually the central area
heated up, melting the ice and becoming our Sun.

*Close to the Sun hot,
rocky protoplanets
formed that became
Mercury and Venus.*

*Ice and rock circling the
Solar System much
farther away from the
Sun eventually collected
into giant planets, such
as Jupiter.*

As the Solar System matured, gravity and the Sun's energy transformed the
material circling around it. Near the center, icy particles melted away,
leaving dry dust that collected into small rocky protoplanets (young planets).
Farther out, bigger protoplanets formed. Far from the Sun, the largest
protoplanets were little more than gas clouds.

**Planets form
from dust and ice**

The Earth warms up

Collisions with other infant planets would have caused hot regions on the Earth's surface, but the Earth probably never glowed like a fiery ball.

4.6 bya A Big Splash makes the Moon

Samples of rock collected by astronauts who landed on the Moon have shown that they are roughly the same age as the oldest rocks on Earth.

The Earth's crust thickens

Until the atmosphere developed, meteorites crashing into the Earth would have given the planet a pockmarked look, like the Moon.

The slow movement of the continents is caused by convection (heat) currents that flow within the liquid rocks of the Earth's mantle.

Pangaea

Today

Photographs from satellites have made us familiar with the shape of the present-day world.

Our Earth formed somewhere between the rocky protoplanets near the Sun and the dirty ice protoplanets farther out. The Earth started small and cool, but it got bigger. The more massive the Earth became, the more gravity squeezed the Earth's core, heating it up. Eventually, much of the planet Earth melted.

A collision with another body the size of Mars caused a huge explosion on the Earth. Dubbed the "Big Splash," the impact threw a huge blob of matter into space. Trapped by gravity in orbit around the Earth, the lump cooled to form our Moon. About 4.6 billion years ago, the Earth began to evolve into the planet that is our home today.

As the temperature dropped, the mass of the Earth separated into layers. The outside of the Earth solidified, forming a solid crust. Wafer thin at first, the crust eventually thickened. As long as the temperature remained above 212°F (100°C), there was no water on the Earth's crust. Water vapor that escaped from the mantle never cooled enough to fall as rain.

After more cooling, the Earth's temperature had fallen far enough for water to collect, instead of boiling off. Rain fell, and seas began to form. Over the years, water eroded the Earth's crust, creating soil. Volcanoes spewed out lava and hot gases. The gases, mainly carbon dioxide and sulfur dioxide, collected as the Earth's atmosphere. Beneath this cloak life began, and the first plants added oxygen to the atmosphere.

Though the Earth's crust is solid, it is not fixed rigidly, and the land masses have drifted to their present positions and shapes over millions of years. About 500 million years ago, six continents ringed the Earth roughly on the equator. Over the next 275 million years, they drifted together to form a super-continent, Pangaea. Since that time, the continents have drifted apart, and they continue to move today.

Modern technology has provided humans with unrivaled power to control life on our planet. Nevertheless, natural disasters quickly demonstrate how weak human beings are. To understand just how insignificant we are, imagine all the processes shown here compressed into one year. The Big Bang created the Universe at midnight on New Year's Day. The Earth formed at the end of September. Dinosaurs didn't appear until about December 26, and became extinct within four days. People arrived last of all, putting in an appearance just eight minutes before midnight on the last day of the year.

FORMATION OF EARTH'S FEATURES

Plate tectonics

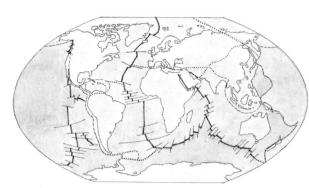

When the Earth's crust cooled and stabilized, it formed tectonic (structural) plates of solid rock. The plates drifted slowly on the Earth's liquid mantle and continue to do so. Where they move together, new mountains form. Where the plates move apart, magma rises to fill the gap.

Volcano chain

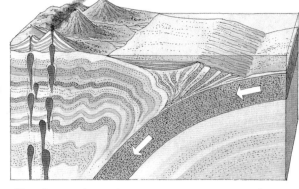

On the coastlines of some continents, an ocean plate meets and slides under a continental plate. At the margin, a deep ocean trench forms. The ocean plate melts as it sinks, creating a line of volcanic mountains (such as South America's Andes) on the continent.

Volcano types

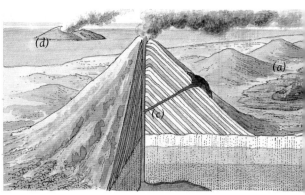

Holes in the Earth's solid crust allow the mantle to escape, forming volcanoes. Active volcanoes take many forms, depending on the gas content of the magma (liquid rock) and how runny it is. Very runny magma gently spreads in a flat sheet forming a shield volcano (a).

Ocean formation

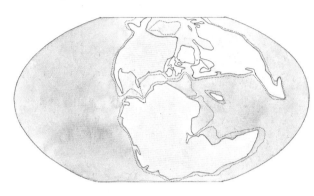

The oceans in their present form began some 225 million years ago. Then, all the land masses formed a super-continent, called Pangaea. As the continental plates drifted apart, low regions between them filled with water that had condensed from vapor in the atmosphere.

Water cycle

The Sun's heat evaporates ocean water, making the air humid (moist). When the air cools or humidity rises, clouds, made of tiny water droplets and ice crystals, form. Rain and snow falling from the clouds collects and flows in rivers to the sea, and the water cycle begins again.

Life of a river

Rain falling on land erodes rock and soil. Some washes into tiny, fast-flowing streams that join to form rivers. Where rivers cross bands of hard rock, waterfalls form, and a river may cut a steep-sided gorge when it flows through areas of low rainfall. As it approaches the sea, a river's flow

Ice ages

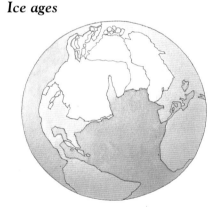

When the Earth's climate was colder, polar ice caps were much bigger than they are today: Arctic ice covered much of Europe and North America. The most recent ice age ended only 10,000 years ago.

Glacial features

From the polar ice caps, and from frozen mountaintops, glaciers spread out across the land. Like rainfall and ocean waves, a glacier erodes the land and carries the rock and soil it removes. When the ice melts, the glacier drops its load. Away from the ice caps, glaciers form below mountain summits, where snow collects. The weight of the snow turns lower layers to ice, and the mass of ice moves slowly downhill at 40 in (one meter) or less a day. Glaciers freeze to the rock they flow over, plucking out chunks as they move on. The accumulated rock collects in a moraine at the glacier's edge.

Mountain building

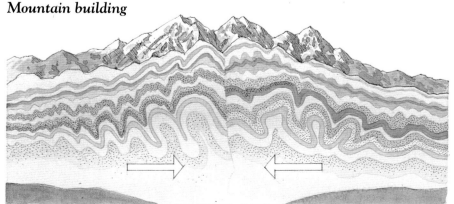

Movement of the Earth's tectonic plates can create vast mountain ranges if the plates collide on a continent. The crust material collects and thickens as the plates move together, faulting (cracking) and folding the rocks. The best known example is the Himalayas in southwestern Asia. About 25 million years ago, northward movement of the plate on which India sits pushed up this mountainous region.

Faulting

Movement deep within the Earth's hot crust usually makes the rock bend or flow. Nearer the surface the rock is brittler, and movement causes faults: cracking and slipping sideways or up and down.

The Earth's layers

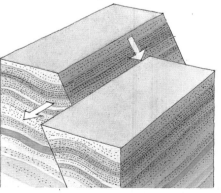

The layers of most rock show how and when it formed. Each layer was once almost horizontal. The lower the layer, the older the rock. Movements of the Earth's crust distort and fold the layers.

Volcanic plug

A church crowns the plug at Le Puy, France.

Marble quarry

Basalt columns

When the magma is sticky and holds lots of gas, the volcano erupts explosively (b). Tall volcanoes (called composite cones) (c) form when liquid magma flows out over the ash ejected in an explosive eruption.

Such activity also forms cauldronlike hot springs and, when an ocean floor volcano erupts, volcanic islands (d). Hawaiian island eruption formations include effusive (e) and caldera (f).

Cooling magma forms hard igneous rock. If softer surrounding rock is washed away, igneous rock may remain as a plug or neck.

The heat and pressure of volcanic activity transforms some other types of rock, turning limestone into denser, harder marble.

When magma cools quickly near the surface, it can form dramatic columns, like this one in the Giant's Causeway, Ireland.

Coastal formation

Sedimentary rocks

(a)

(b)

(c)

Most of the Earth's water is in the oceans, and only a tiny amount in rivers. If the oceans were drained tomorrow, the rivers would take 37,000 years to refill them.

slows. Its valley spreads and flattens and it drops some of its soil load as it floods across the flat plain where it flows out into the sea. This forms a delta, a low-lying island or group of islands made of sediments, at the river's mouth.

The ocean's constant pounding carves caves, coves, cliffs, and arches from the shore. When an arch collapses, it leaves an isolated stack. The waves carry away the rock they cut from the land, and usually deposit it not far away. The sand and shingle collects as beaches, bars, and spits.

On the ocean bed, sedimentary rocks form in three ways: dissolved salts form crystals (a); sediment sinks (b); or the skeletons of animals such as coral polyps collect in layers (c). Sedimentary rocks have preserved the fossilized bones of many creatures.

When the ice melts

Ice caps

Iceberg

When glaciers melt, they leave behind traces. Bowl-shaped cirques show where the ice first collected. A small stream flows down the huge U-shaped valley that the glacier smoothed and enlarged. Rocks caught in the ice sometimes leave long grooves in the valley floor.

Today the Earth still has two ice caps, but they are much smaller than they were in the ice ages. At the South Pole, the permanent ice is up to 6,500 ft (2,000 m) thick, and covers a continent – Antarctica. In the north, drifting ice floats 16-23 ft (5-7 m) thick on the Arctic ocean; much melts in summer.

When the glaciers of Greenland and Antarctica reach the sea, chunks break off to form icebergs. Some are bigger than Belgium. Icebergs melt and break up as they float into warmer water, but they can tower 500 ft (150 m) high, with six times more ice under the water.

Earthquakes

Wind erosion

Mountain features

Pressure along fault lines builds for a long time before the fault suddenly slips. Then an earthquake shakes the ground, often creating deep cracks in the rock and destroying buildings. Some 6,000 earthquakes take place each year, but only 15 or so kill people or cause damage.

In dry regions wind helps shape the landscape. Wind can move only particles 1/12 in (2 mm) in diameter or smaller, but by removing soft rock under a harder boulder, the wind sculpts strange landforms.

Bare rock is usually visible only on steep mountain slopes where rain washes away weathered stone. Lower down, weathered rock forms a layer of soil that supports tiny plants. Lower still, hardy evergreen trees grow with downward-sloping boughs that shrug off snow. Broad-leaved forests flourish only on low slopes and in valleys.

ORIGINS OF LIFE

3.8 billion years ago Life began

The first living things

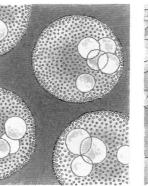

Stromatolites

Single-celled animals

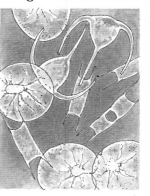

Nobody really knows how life began on Earth. Many believe that lightning strikes caused the elements carbon, hydrogen, and oxygen in the world's oceans to combine. These reactions would have created simple molecules that in turn could have combined to form DNA – the basic building block of life. An alternative theory is that a meteorite brought the first organic material to Earth.

Bacteria were probably the first form of life, forming more than 3.5 billion years ago. The first plants – blue-green algae – followed.

In shallow oceans, algae grew into large dome-shaped mats. Preserved in stone as fossils, these algae are called stromatolites.

Around the same time, protozoa, meaning "first animals," appeared. Made of just one cell, they were microscopically small.

500-425 mya Ordovician sea life

Graptolites

First fish

Two thin, bony plates form skull

425-400 mya Silurian plants

Trilobites were also common in the Ordovician Period. They shared the warm seas with squidlike nautiloids and with brachiopods, which resembled modern clams. Corals flourished too, along with other simple invertebrates such as bryozoans, which created elegant twiglike structures from their calcium shells. Fossils of tiny invertebrate graptolites look like saw blades pressed into rock.

Vertebrates – animals with backbones – evolved in the Ordovician Period. The first was *Arandapsis*, a jawless fish. The lamprey and hagfish are its modern-day descendants.

The first land plants appeared toward the end of the Silurian Period, about 400 million years ago. The earliest plants were similar to the whisk fern of today. Tiny mosses probably evolved from them.

400-340 mya Devonian fish

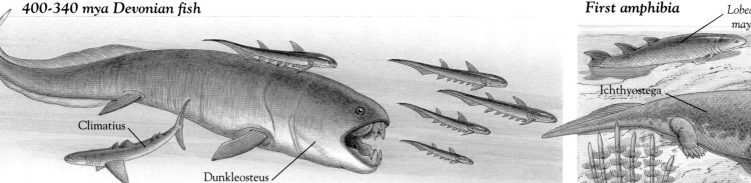

Climatius

Dunkleosteus

First amphibia

Lobed-finned Eusthenopteron may have been the ancestor of the first amphibia.

Ichthyostega

The Devonian Period, which lasted for some 60 million years, has been called "the age of the fish" because the Devonian oceans swarmed with life. Not only were there more fish than in earlier periods, but there was also a greater variety. Descendants of primitive jawless fish had to fight for space and food with frightening predators, such as *Dunkleosteus*. From the tip of its eellike tail to the ferocious jaws on its heavily armored head, this fish measured up to 11 ft 6 in (3.5 m) in length.

Fish literally took a remarkable step forward in the late Devonian Period: they stepped from ocean to land. First to accomplish this was *Ichthyostega*. It became the world's first amphibian, at home in water and on land, and able to breathe air through its moist skin surface.

280 mya Eryops

270 mya Dimetrodon

225 mya Chasmatosaurus

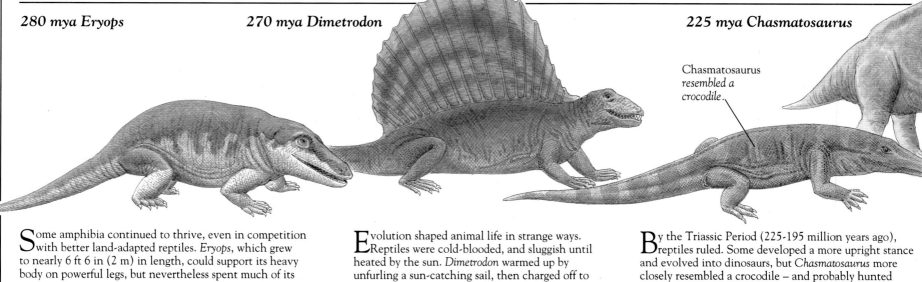

Chasmatosaurus resembled a crocodile.

Some amphibia continued to thrive, even in competition with better land-adapted reptiles. *Eryops*, which grew to nearly 6 ft 6 in (2 m) in length, could support its heavy body on powerful legs, but nevertheless spent much of its time in water.

Evolution shaped animal life in strange ways. Reptiles were cold-blooded, and sluggish until heated by the sun. *Dimetrodon* warmed up by unfurling a sun-catching sail, then charged off to eat less well-equipped reptiles.

By the Triassic Period (225-195 million years ago), reptiles ruled. Some developed a more upright stance and evolved into dinosaurs, but *Chasmatosaurus* more closely resembled a crocodile – and probably hunted in a similar way.

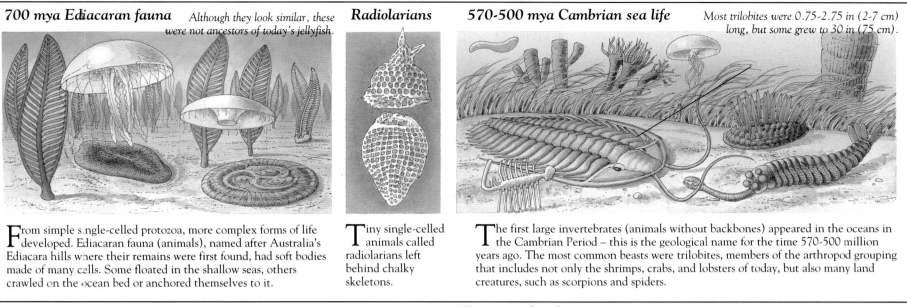

700 mya Ediacaran fauna *Although they look similar, these were not ancestors of today's jellyfish.*

Radiolarians

570-500 mya Cambrian sea life *Most trilobites were 0.75-2.75 in (2-7 cm) long, but some grew to 30 in (75 cm).*

From simple single-celled protozoa, more complex forms of life developed. Ediacaran fauna (animals), named after Australia's Ediacara hills where their remains were first found, had soft bodies made of many cells. Some floated in the shallow seas, others crawled on the ocean bed or anchored themselves to it.

Tiny single-celled animals called radiolarians left behind chalky skeletons.

The first large invertebrates (animals without backbones) appeared in the oceans in the Cambrian Period – this is the geological name for the time 570-500 million years ago. The most common beasts were trilobites, members of the arthropod grouping that includes not only the shrimps, crabs, and lobsters of today, but also many land creatures, such as scorpions and spiders.

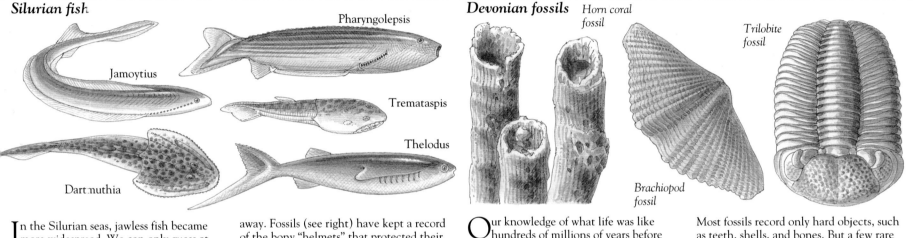

Silurian fish

Pharyngolepis

Jamoytius

Tremataspis

Thelodus

Dartmuthia

Devonian fossils *Horn coral fossil*

Trilobite fossil

Brachiopod fossil

In the Silurian seas, jawless fish became more widespread. We can only guess at the body shape of these fish because their skeletons were made not from true bone, but from soft cartilage, which has rotted away. Fossils (see right) have kept a record of the bony "helmets" that protected their heads. The fossils also show that they were under 12 in (0.3 m) long and had few fins, so they were probably poor swimmers.

Our knowledge of what life was like hundreds of millions of years before the first humans evolved comes from fossils. These are the remains of prehistoric creatures and plants preserved in rocks.

Most fossils record only hard objects, such as teeth, shells, and bones. But a few rare fossils also record delicate structures such as feathers through a process similar to plaster casting.

300 mya Carboniferous reptiles

Dinosaur ancestor Petrolacosaurus

Hylonomus was the first reptile.

Swamp forests of the Carboniferous Period

Devonian amphibia laid soft eggs in water, like today's frogs. But after 100 million years, reptiles evolved, and began to lay their leathery eggs on land. Reptiles were better adapted for land life in other ways, too: they had horny scales on their bodies rather than moist skin; and their lungs were more efficient.

Other animals and plants had been evolving just as fast as the reptiles, and all but the most hostile regions of the Earth supported life during the Carboniferous Period (340-280 million years ago). Coniferous trees shaded lush ferns and rushes on the swampy forest floors. Tree-ferns grew to great heights, too. As plants died and the tree trunks crashed into the swamps, their woody remains formed the coal and oil that now fuels cars and power stations.

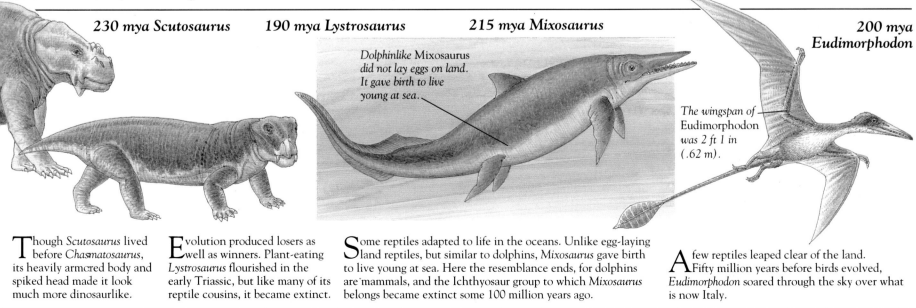

230 mya Scutosaurus   **190 mya Lystrosaurus**   **215 mya Mixosaurus**

Dolphinlike Mixosaurus did not lay eggs on land. It gave birth to live young at sea.

200 mya Eudimorphodon

The wingspan of Eudimorphodon was 2 ft 1 in (.62 m).

Though *Scutosaurus* lived before *Chasmatosaurus*, its heavily armored body and spiked head made it look much more dinosaurlike.

Evolution produced losers as well as winners. Plant-eating *Lystrosaurus* flourished in the early Triassic, but like many of its reptile cousins, it became extinct.

Some reptiles adapted to life in the oceans. Unlike egg-laying land reptiles, but similar to dolphins, *Mixosaurus* gave birth to live young at sea. Here the resemblance ends, for dolphins are mammals, and the Ichthyosaur group to which *Mixosaurus* belongs became extinct some 100 million years ago.

A few reptiles leaped clear of the land. Fifty million years before birds evolved, *Eudimorphodon* soared through the sky over what is now Italy.

Dinosaurs

| 360-210 million years ago (mya) Amphibians | 320-215 mya Reptiles | 230 mya Herrerasaurus | 215 mya Massospondylus | 215 mya Coelophysis |

The ancestors of the dinosaur were the amphibians. They bred in water, and their young lived much like fish. As they grew, they developed lungs and legs, so they could breathe air and crawl on land.

Some amphibians evolved into reptiles: they grew scales, they had stronger lungs, and they laid leathery eggs on land. Dinosaurs evolved from the most successful later reptiles, the thecodonts.

One of the earliest of the dinosaurs, *Herrerasaurus*, stalked the region that is now South America (though this continent was then joined to Africa). It was a 10-ft (3-m) long flesh-eating dinosaur.

The 13-ft (4-m) long *Massospondylus* was one of the more common dinosaurs in southern Africa. Its contemporary was the agile *Coelophysis*, who stalked the banks of lakes in upland forests, eating small game.

140 mya Stegosaurus

Large horny plates

140 mya Compsognathus

Whiplash tail for defense

140 mya Apatosaurus (Brontosaurus)

Darting around the woodlands of what is now France and Germany, chicken-sized *Compsognathus* was a skilled hunter. It could probably run at speeds of up to 25 mph (40 km/h).

The *Stegosaurus* may have developed horny back-plates to discourage predators, but the plates had a network of veins, so the dinosaur may also have used them to keep cool. *Stegosaurus* was 25 ft (7.7 m) long.

Weighing in at 33 tons (30 tonnes), *Apatosaurus* shook the ground when it walked. If attacked, its teeth were useless for fighting; *Apatosaurus* probably relied on its tail as a weapon.

130 mya Brachiosaurus

120 mya Baryonyx

Huge claws

120 mya Archaeopteryx

110 mya Iguanodon

Fossils of the enormous *Brachiosaurus* record that it roamed what is now Europe, Africa, and America. It was one of the largest animals ever to walk the Earth, yet it was a placid plant eater.

Found in England, *Baryonyx* was equipped with huge claws and a long, crocodilelike skull. Fish remains found with the beast's fossil suggest that it may have used its claws to fish in rivers.

Pigeon-sized *Archaeopteryx* provides the only known link between dinosaurs and modern birds. Though it had a wishbone like a bird, it lacked strong wings, and may only have used them for gliding.

An *Iguanodon* shinbone found in England in 1809 was only the second dinosaur fossil to be unearthed anywhere. Early attempts to recreate the ancient animal were wildly inaccurate.

65 mya Saltasaurus

Bony plates

Head crest

65 mya Ankylosaurus

Thick armor plating

65 mya Parasaurolophus

Club tail

Bony plates covered the back and sides of *Saltasaurus*. The scaly armor would have been flexible enough to allow the dinosaur to move freely, yet strong enough to provide protection against predators.

The spectacular crest of *Parasaurolophus* was hollow and connected to its nose, so this dinosaur possibly had a low-pitched, haunting call. In forests, the beast may have tucked its crest into a notch on its back,

using the arching crest to deflect low branches. Part of the Hadrosaur family, *Parasaurolophus* had a ducklike bill. In its mouth it had many teeth for grinding down the plants on which it fed.

The most heavily armored of all dinosaurs, *Ankylosaurus* was built like a tank, and at 20 ft (6 m) long, it was as big as one! If attacked, it probably curled up, but it could also use its clublike tail to fight back.

215 mya Plateosaurus

200 mya Lesothosaurus

150 mya Mamenchisaurus

140 mya Tuojiangosaurus

Spiky tail

The long neck of *Plateosaurus* enabled it to nibble succulent leaves near the tops of tall trees.

Home for *Lesothosaurus* was a dry plain of southern Africa. There this turkey-sized animal probably chased its quarry at some speed. It burrowed in the hot season, preferring to hunt in cooler weather.

Nearly half of the *Mamenchisaurus's* 72-ft (22-m) length was its neck. When it stood on tiptoe, its extraordinary neck allowed it to reach the tops of the conifer trees in the forests where it lived.

Plant-eating *Tuojiangosaurus* lived in China about 140 million years ago. It had rows of bony plates on its back, and could have put an attacking predator out of action with a blow from its spiked tail.

130 mya Allosaurus

130 mya Ceratosaurus

Horn on nose

130 mya Camarasaurus

Long neck

The main predator of the *Apatosaurus* was only a seventh of its size and weight: the *Allosaurus* had greater mobility and ferocious teeth, which more than compensated for its size disadvantage.

Like a rhino, *Ceratosaurus* had a bony horn. Too small to be useful in a fight, the horn may have played a part in the dinosaur's mating display.

The *Camarasaurus* breathed through large openings on the top of its skull, and some scientists suggest that the dinosaur was equipped with an elephant-like trunk. However, even without this, the

60-foot (18-m) long animal had no difficulty feeding on the lower boughs of pine trees. *Camarasaurus* means "chambered lizard" and refers to the hollow spaces in its bones, which reduced its weight.

110 mya Hypsilophodon

100 mya Spinosaurus

Skin "sail"

80 mya Deinonychus

80 mya Protoceratops

75 mya Oviraptor

Razor-sharp slashing claw

The *Hypsilophodon* flourished in what is now Europe and North America. Browsing on trees and small plants, family groups of *Hypsilophodon* were always alert. They relied on speed to escape predators.

Nobody knows for sure why *Spinosaurus* grew a large "sail" on its back. It may have caught the sun, to warm the animal's blood, or the wind, to cool it.

Ferocious *Deinonychus* was a formidable predator. It had a large brain and a sharp, 5-in (13-cm) long claw on each of its back legs. To attack, *Deinonychus* probably stood on one leg and slashed out at its victim.

The discovery of *Protoceratops* nests with eggs showed that this dinosaur cared for its young. It would have had to constantly be on guard for *Oviraptor*, a dinosaur whose name means "egg thief."

65 mya Triceratops

Bony frill

65 mya Pachycephalosaurus

65 mya Gallimimus

Bony helmet

65 mya Tyrannosaurus

Ostrichlike legs

The last of the meat-eating dinosaurs to evolve, *Tyrannosaurus* was also the largest, growing to 50 ft (15 m). Though fearsome, *Tyrannosaurus* was clumsy, and its front legs were almost useless.

Heavier than a modern male elephant, *Triceratops* had three horns for attack and a bony frill for defense. Fighting over females was probably common behavior: many fossil frills are damaged and scarred.

Competing for partners like mountain goats, *Pachycephalosaurus* males may have head-butted each other. Little wonder, then, that they developed a domed "crash helmet" of bone on the tops of their skulls.

With a beak and birdlike habits, *Gallimimus* resembled a modern ostrich. It was one of the last of the dinosaurs, and like all the others, *Gallimimus* became extinct 65 million years ago. Nobody knows why for sure.

MAMMALS

300-280 mya Archaeothyris

Cynognathus looked more like a mammal than a lizard.

Archaeothyris resembled a lizard.

Among the earliest of the mammallike reptiles, *Archaeothyris* looked much like a lizard. The creature's wide jaws and varied teeth suggest that it was as happy ripping flesh as it was chewing leaves.

245-230 mya Cynognathus

Doglike jaws

This wolf-sized beast was a direct ancestor of mammals. *Cynognathus* may have been hairy, or scaly like its reptile cousins. It walked more like a mammal than a lizard and had doglike jaws.

205-175 mya Megazostrodon

An ancestor of the duck-billed platypus

The shrewlike *Megazostrodon* probably laid leathery eggs. It lived in what is now Africa and was 5 in (12 cm) long. Monotremes, such as the duck-billed platypus, are its direct modern descendants.

135-115 mya Crusafontia

Like its close relatives, this primitive ancestor of today's mammals may have been squirrellike. It's impossible to know for sure, because paleontologists have only found one tooth!

40 mya Sarkastodon

Bearlike body characteristics

Cats, dogs, and seals had the same ancestors as this 10-ft (3-m) long meat eater. However, the Creodont order to which it belonged died out 7 mya, and *Sarkastodon* has no modern descendants.

35 mya Palaeolagus

Short legs better for running than hopping

Small gnawing mammals, the Lagomorpha order includes today's hares, rabbits, and pikas. *Palaeolagus*, the first lagomorph, had shorter legs than a rabbit. It probably ran rather than hopped.

35-30 mya Embolotherium

The huge "horn" that juts from the snout of 8-ft (2.5-m) high *Embolotherium* was actually made of skin-covered bone. It left little room for a brain, so this plant eater was most likely not a deep thinker.

35-25 mya Hesperocyon

Good hearing, sharp eyes, and a keen sense of smell helped the canid family compete. *Hesperocyon*, one of the first canids to evolve, looks more like a weasel than the dogs that descended from it.

25-5 mya Rytiodus

Rytiodus looked much like a sea lion, but was a plant eater.

Rytiodus ate plants and may have shared a common ancestor with the Proboscidean order, which includes the modern elephant. *Rytiodus* evolved into the modern dugong, or sea cow.

10-5 mya Procamelus

Back hump not developed yet

This ancestor of the camel was not as specialized as the modern beast. Though it lacks a fatty hump on the back, *Procamelus* has the same splaying toes to support its weight on soft ground.

5-10 mya Platybelodon

Prominent flat tusks used to shovel up weeds from shallow water

The similarity between *Platybelodon* and elephants is hard to miss. It pulled up weeds from shallow water using its tusks, but such a specialized feeding method made the beast vulnerable to competition.

3.5 mya Canis dirus

Canis dirus was probably a scavenger.

The dire wolf closely resembled the modern wolf, but at 6 ft 6 in (2 m) long, it was bigger. Like *Hesperocyon* in the row above, *Canis dirus* shared ancestors with the cat.

60-50 mya Plesiadapis

The primate order to which humans belong evolved from insect-eating mammals some 60 million years ago. One of the very earliest primates, *Plesiadapis* looked more like a squirrel than an ape.

33 mya Propliopithecus

Though it became extinct within 25 million years, this ape could have been the evolutionary link from the earlier lemurlike primates to the later types from which modern primates are descended.

16-9 mya Dryopithecus

The tree ape *Dryopithecus* could walk on its hind legs, though it was more comfortable on all fours. It was probably a direct ancestor of chimps and gorillas.

5.5-2.5 mya   *Australopithecus afarensis*

This creature of the distant past had an apelike face, but walked upright. Its remains were found in the Afar region of Ethiopia – hence the name, "Southern ape from Afar."

100-75 mya Marsupials

Diprotodon

Argyrolagus *looked similar to a kangaroo.*

Marsupials are the oldest true mammals. Like modern kangaroos, the 10-ft (3-m) long *Diprotodon* carried its young in a pouch; the 16-in (40-cm) *Argyrolagus* more closely resembled its Australian descendant.

55-50 mya Hyracotherium

Dog-sized Hyracotherium

Remains of the first horse-like mammals have been found in Wyoming and Utah. *Hyracotherium* was related to today's tapirs and rhinos.

55-50 mya Ischyromys

Ischyromys

The first rodents looked like mice, but possibly lived like squirrels. Their offspring evolved into rats, squirrels, and mice.

50 mya Icaronycteris

Fossils of this flying mammal were so complete that scientists could tell what it dined on. *Icaronycteris* ate insects on the wing.

45 mya Protocetus

Limbs resemble land mammals

Modern whales, dolphins, and porpoises probably all evolved from land mammals about 65 mya. *Protocetus* looked like a modern whale, but its limbs were still like those of land mammals.

25-20 mya Miotapirus

Snout suited to foraging on forest floor

Even after millions of years of evolution the present day tapir is still very similar to its ancestor *Miotapirus*. Growing to 6 ft 6 in (2 m) long, this piglike animal foraged at night in tropical forests.

25-15 mya Moropus

Head shaped like a horse

Catlike claws

With the claws of a cat, the teeth of a cow, and head of a horse, *Moropus* was like a mammal designed by a government department. This 10-ft (3-m) tall beast lived in North America.

25-10 mya Homalodotherium

Homalodotherium stood on its hind legs to browse trees.

As big as a human adult, this South American mammal belongs to the *notoungulate* order of mammals that also includes small, rabbitlike creatures.

25-5 mya Desmostylus

A typical seaworthy carnivore, *Desmostylus* was a little like a modern hippo. Cumbersome on land, it propelled itself along in shallow water by walking on the muddy bottom.

3-1 mya Metridiochoerus

Metridiochoerus ate both plants and meat.

This giant African warthog was not fussy. It greedily guzzled both plants and meat, just like the domestic pig. The suborder Suina, to which both belong, also includes the hippo and peccary.

2 mya Ursus spelaeus

The cave bear looked a lot like its descendant, the modern bear. At 6 ft 6 in (2 m) long, it was one of the largest of the Carnivora order that included cats, dogs, stoats, weasels, and otters.

1 mya Smilodon

Ancestor of both domestic cats and big wild cats

This saber-toothed cat preyed on large clumsy mammals. It was a member of the Felidae family from which both tigers and panthers (big cats) and the domestic cat are descended.

1 mya-12,000 years ago Pelorovis

Related to the modern African buffalo, *Pelorovis* was a vast beast with horns perhaps 13 ft (4 m) across. It shared the same evolutionary roots as present-day giraffes, deer, and cattle.

2-1.5 mya Homo habilis

The first tool-using human was called *Homo habilis*, which means "handy human." Adept at making use of basic tools such as flints, these humans may even have developed the power of speech.

1.6 mya -200,000 years ago Homo erectus

A "true" human, *Homo erectus* (upright person) learned how to use refined tools and how to use fire for defense and cooking. This successful hominid wandered from Africa to southern Europe and Asia.

250,000 years ago Neanderthals

Neanderthal people originated in Germany, living 250,000-30,000 years ago. They were almost as intelligent as modern people. Communities buried their dead, suggesting they had religious beliefs.

35,000 years ago Homo sapiens sapiens

The evolution of modern humans was more or less complete some 400 centuries ago. Since then *Homo sapiens sapiens* has dominated our planet and all other animal species.

EVERYDAY LIFE

IN THE BEGINNING ...
PEOPLE'S BASIC NEEDS WERE MUCH THE SAME AS THOSE WE HAVE TODAY.

Simple but deadly weapons

BECAUSE THEY HAD TO KEEP WARM, EARLY PEOPLE MADE CLOTHING. THEY NEEDED TO KEEP OUT THE RAIN AND WIND, SO THEY BUILT SHELTERS. WITH THE FIRST SIMPLE WEAPONS – STONES AND CLUBS – THEY DEFENDED THEMSELVES AGAINST WILD BEASTS OR KILLED THEM FOR FOOD. WITH MEDICINE people guarded against disease and injury. Look closer, though, and it's clear that time has changed everyday life beyond all recognition.

Clothing made using animal skins

30,000 YEARS AGO

HOMO SAPIENS WAS THE MOST SUCCESSFUL SPECIES ON EARTH WHEN IT EVOLVED, AND IT COLONIZED ALMOST ALL HABITABLE REGIONS. These early people reached islands, such as Japan, when the oceans froze or when sea levels were low enough to form land bridges. Dressed in skins, they lived out uncomfortable lives in shelters of branches or bones. They made simple stone and horn weapons that brought them dangerously close to a snorting, often ferocious, lunch. And healers relied on prayer and superstition for cures.

Mammoth tusks support roof

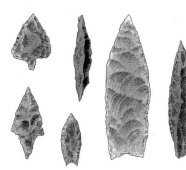

Arrowheads and spear points

Flint working

3,000 YEARS AGO

THE FIRST CITY CIVILIZATIONS FLOURISHED ON THE BANKS OF A few great rivers: the Nile, Tigris, and Euphrates. For most people, everyday life was still a desperate, squalid struggle against disease and starvation. But for a wealthy few, everyday life had a leisurely pace – they lived in elaborate multiroom houses and wore elegant garments that signaled their status. In the Egypt of the pharaohs, doctors performed surgery to remove tumors. Weapons, deadly against wild animals, were often aimed at people.

Scribes of the Indus Valley (now Pakistan)

Egyptian chariot

300 YEARS AGO

IN THE 1600s AFRICAN SLAVES WERE WORKED BRUTALLY TO HARVEST ABUNDANT SUGARCANE CROPS IN THE CARIBBEAN. The sugar they extracted made life sweeter in Europe. There, in elegant town houses, wealthy men wearing huge powdered wigs stirred sugar into their coffee. Decorative swords hung from their belts, but for dueling or hunting they probably chose flintlock pistols or muskets. Even after 27 centuries, there was still no understanding of, or cure for, infection.

London town houses

Flintlock weapons

30 YEARS AGO

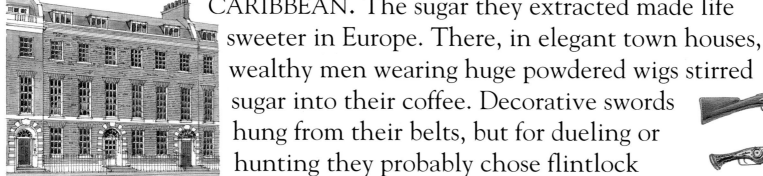

IN INDUSTRIALIZED WESTERN NATIONS, EVERYDAY life had more or less evolved into its present-day form by the mid-twentieth century. Modern doctors had become better at warding off death, but the world's superpowers had enough nuclear missiles to end everyday life forever. They still do.

Modern high-rise housing

Performing surgery using a microscope

HOMES

750,000 BC *Caves*

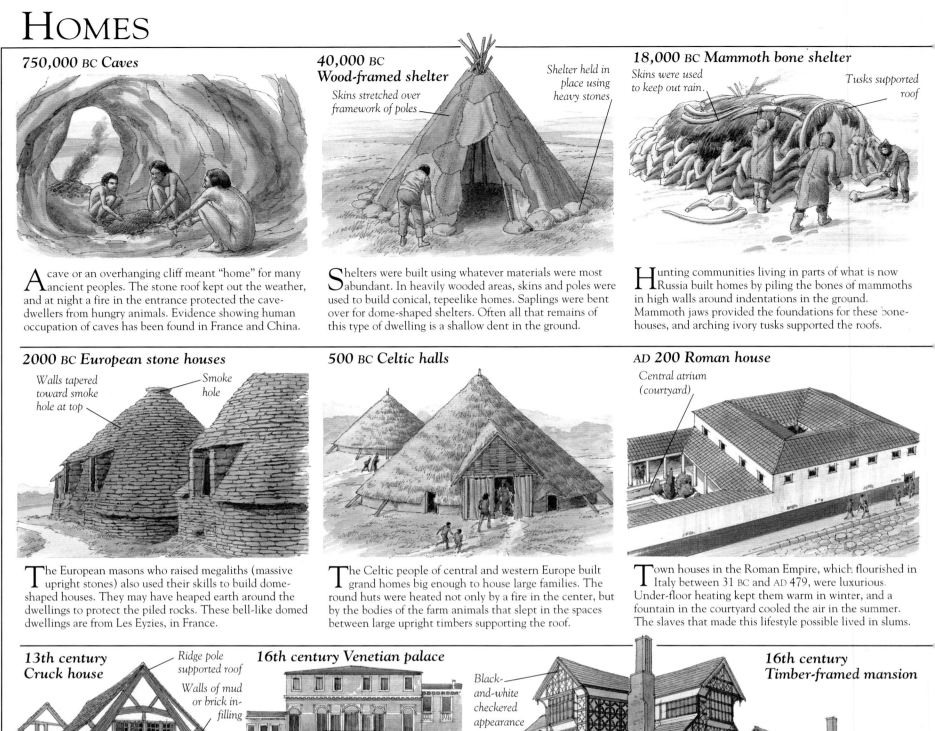

A cave or an overhanging cliff meant "home" for many ancient peoples. The stone roof kept out the weather, and at night a fire in the entrance protected the cave-dwellers from hungry animals. Evidence showing human occupation of caves has been found in France and China.

40,000 BC *Wood-framed shelter*

Skins stretched over framework of poles

Shelter held in place using heavy stones

Shelters were built using whatever materials were most abundant. In heavily wooded areas, skins and poles were used to build conical, tepeelike homes. Saplings were bent over for dome-shaped shelters. Often all that remains of this type of dwelling is a shallow dent in the ground.

18,000 BC *Mammoth bone shelter*

Skins were used to keep out rain.

Tusks supported roof

Hunting communities living in parts of what is now Russia built homes by piling the bones of mammoths in high walls around indentations in the ground. Mammoth jaws provided the foundations for these bone-houses, and arching ivory tusks supported the roofs.

2000 BC *European stone houses*

Walls tapered toward smoke hole at top

Smoke hole

The European masons who raised megaliths (massive upright stones) also used their skills to build dome-shaped houses. They may have heaped earth around the dwellings to protect the piled rocks. These bell-like domed dwellings are from Les Eyzies, in France.

500 BC *Celtic halls*

The Celtic people of central and western Europe built grand homes big enough to house large families. The round huts were heated not only by a fire in the center, but by the bodies of the farm animals that slept in the spaces between large upright timbers supporting the roof.

AD 200 *Roman house*

Central atrium (courtyard)

Town houses in the Roman Empire, which flourished in Italy between 31 BC and AD 479, were luxurious. Under-floor heating kept them warm in winter, and a fountain in the courtyard cooled the air in the summer. The slaves that made this lifestyle possible lived in slums.

13th century *Cruck house*

Ridge pole supported roof

Walls of mud or brick in-filling

English cruck houses developed from the Celtic hut. A curved tree was split down the middle, producing two matching posts, or crucks. These were leaned together to make the ends of the house.

16th century *Venetian palace*

Wealthy Venetian traders built grand palaces in the 16th century. Wide arches leading off of canals made a majestic entrance. On the floor above, rows of arched windows kept rooms light and airy.

16th century *Timber-framed mansion*

Black-and-white checkered appearance

By the 16th century, European carpenters could build large timber-framed houses. They constructed a frame of oak at their workshops, then assembled it rapidly where the house was to be built.

Trenells (tree-nails) made of iron-hard oak heartwood held the frame together. Filling the gaps with woven brushwood covered in lime-washed mud produced a black-and-white checkered appearance.

1930s *Prefabricated house*

Influential "Modernist" architects of the early 20th century rejected as dishonest houses decorated in the styles of the past. Instead, they designed with simple shapes, and showed off a building's structure.

Traditional Japanese house

Traditional Japanese houses are the result of centuries of refinement. Built almost entirely of timber, the houses are held together with intricate joints and wooden pegs. Shingles (tiles of split wood) seal the walls and roof, and screens of stretched paper divide the interior into rooms.

1936-8 *Falling Water*

American architect Frank Lloyd Wright (1867-1959) used the same materials as the Modernist architects – concrete, steel, and glass – but he developed a highly individual style. His buildings merged with the landscape and echoed nature. For example, the balcony of his Falling Water house at Bear Run, Pennsylvania, repeats the rock slab below.

7000 BC Çatal Hüyük

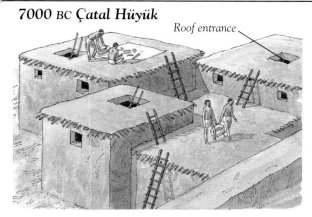

Roof entrance

Houses changed as hunters began to tame animals and food gatherers began to plant seeds. People began to build more permanent homes like these mud-brick houses at Çatal Hüyük in central Turkey. The houses had no doors, so archaeologists guess they had roof entrances.

c.6000 BC Igloo

Large igloos housed entire families.

To the Inuit of the Arctic, an igloo is a house of any kind, though most people use the word to mean a dome-shaped snow-block shelter. There was no fixed size for an igloo: the smallest were shelters that experienced hunters built quickly with only a bone knife.

c.4000 BC Lake dwellings

Marshland and lakes provided safe (though damp) sites for homes. Lake dwellers sank vertical logs into the mud, then built a platform on them well above the water level. People in what is now Switzerland were among the first to build stilt houses like these, some 6,000 years ago.

AD 950 Viking house

Walls made of closely spaced logs

The Nordic people of Scandinavia sailed as far as North America, building houses in a similar style everywhere they went. Where timber was plentiful they used logs, but elsewhere they used stone. Many Viking houses were boat-shaped, with a painted dragon's head over the entrance.

1180 Norman manor house

When William the Conqueror led French troops into England in 1066, he took the Norman style of building with him. For security, the hall of a Norman manor house was on the second floor. Beneath it, an undercroft with a stone ceiling provided fireproof storage.

1200-1400 Pueblo cliff dwellings

The Anasazi people built groups of stone and mud pit houses in the Mesa Verde region of Colorado. The Cliff Palace, built in the shelter of an overhanging rock face, has more than 200 rooms. These amazing houses were abandoned around 1300, perhaps because of drought.

1800 London town house

High land prices forced London's builders to make good use of even tiny plots in the 18th and 19th century. They raised the ground floor of terraced houses and squeezed offices and kitchens into the basement.

19th century Frontier log cabin

In its simplest form, the log cabin of the North American frontier was a makeshift hut of notched logs, roofed with turf. But with squared logs and a shingle roof, settlers could make cabins dry and snug.

1800s North American house

House made entirely of wood

Labeled "Stick-style" because of their thin supporting columns, 19th-century North American suburban houses were quick and inexpensive to construct. They were popular with families fleeing the cities.

20th century English terrace

New streetcars and railroads made daily travel to work easy, so English families also moved out of town, to solidly built brick homes. These houses were small by US standards because land was expensive.

1946-52 Unité d'Habitation

Early high-rise housing, such as Unité d'Habitation by Swiss-French architect Le Corbusier (alias Charles Edouard Jeanneret 1887-1965), contained an assortment of big and small apartments. Integrated community and shopping services made the building a vertical village.

1960s Apartment towers

Other architects built cheap housing by copying the apartment tower style, but leaving out the social services, such as playgrounds, gyms, and theaters. Residents soon grew to hate what they saw as prisons in the clouds.

Suburban home

Outside Western cities, most modern homes are single-family units, often timber-framed, built in neighborhoods. Developers sometimes cover the house in a superficial skin of brick, tile, or shingles to make it look traditional.

CLOTHING

Early people
In cool regions, early peoples made clothes from animal skins crudely stitched with hide thongs.

2900 BC Sumer
Animal skins
Wool
Sumerians combed and twisted wool into a pattern of tufts to decorate their fur garments.

1500 BC Egypt
Simple linen kilt
Ancient Egyptian men and women worked naked or wore a linen kilt. All used makeup for protection against insects and sun.

1350 BC Egypt
Wig
Egyptian nobles had fine jewelry and elaborate clothes. Women painted their faces and put ointment into their elaborate wigs.

1000 BC Nubia
Draped loincloth
Warriors of Nubia (a land on the Nile River south of Egypt) fought in Egyptian armies wearing only a draped loincloth.

700 BC Assyria
Coat sewn with metal plates
Over the short tunic worn by working Assyrians, warriors wore a linen coat sewn with metal plates and a conical helmet.

1st century AD Afghanistan
Sewn furs
Afghanistani people wore sewn furs, skin side out. In an extreme climate they kept out the cold, but were easy to take off in hot sun.

4th century AD Rome
Imported silk and cotton fabrics
As the Roman Empire grew, imported fabrics replaced the heavy wool of the toga. Most people wore lighter clothes for informal occasions.

Central America
Feathers
In Central America the Mayan people wore few clothes, except at festivals. Then, colorful feathers enlivened hats and skirts.

Byzantine Empire
Elaborate clothing
European and Asian cultures influenced the clothing styles of the Byzantine Empire. Wealthy people of Constantinople (Istanbul) wore gold, gems, and elegant clothes of luxurious and colorful fabrics.

Norse people
Breeches (pants)
Northern European clothing was a simpler affair. Over linen underwear, men wore breeches (pants), and women a long dress. Heavy brooches fixed cloaks.

15th century Italy
Wealthy Italian merchants flaunted their riches in fabulous clothes made from costly Oriental textiles.

Netherlands
Deep pleats
These wedding clothes are just as extravagant. Deep pleating and fur trimmings show that the pair are rich.

Russia
Fur-lined coat
Styles of Russian clothes varied widely. In the frozen north both men and women wore an ankle length coat, fur-lined in winter.

16th century England
Padded shoulders
Flat hat
A 16th-century gentleman padded his shoulders and wore a flat hat. His wife wore a figure-hugging bodice and hood.

India
When the Moguls came to India from their native Afghanistan, they introduced a pleated skirt worn over muslin pants.

Spain
Pleated skirt
Gold from America made Spain the richest European nation. Spanish styles influenced tailors all over the Old World.

1700s England
Fashionable three-cornered fur hats led to the slaughter of millions of beavers for their fur.

North America
Cravat
North America's fashions were similar to Europe's: the cravat (a knotted handkerchief) was to lead to the necktie.

North Africa
In Islamic countries, tradition insisted – as it does today – that women hide their faces behind a veil.

England
Metal hoops held up English women's skirts. To walk through doors, the wearer had to turn sideways.

France
In revolutionary France, aristocrats cut their long hair at the neck to mourn those whose necks the guillotine cut.

19th century France
Silk top hats became the fashion for men at the start of the 19th century, just saving the beaver from extinction.

North America
Frontier clothing had to be tough. In the cities, some women copied Amelia Bloomer and wore baggy pants, or bloomers.

700 BC Babylon

Long, fringed tunic

Babylonian nobility wore fringed tunics shaped to imitate animal skins.

500 BC Parthia

Parthians (Persians) wore loose-fitting tunics, tied at the waist with a belt or two.

Greece

Long, flowing chiton

The chiton of the early Greeks was not sewn. Knots or pins held it together.

Greek wars

Greek armor hugged the body. Rippling muscles decorated the breastplate.

Susa

The clothing of the temple guards of Susa (SW Iran) was splendid, but hardly soldierly.

200 BC China

Steel-plate armor

Chinese soldiers of the Chi'in dynasty wore armor 17 centuries before its use in Europe.

Rome

Toga *Stola*

Early Roman clothing was modeled on Greek flowing robes: men wore a toga, and women, a stola.

Ethiopia

A lion-skin cape – complete with the tail – identified high-ranking people in Ethiopia.

11th century Norman

Mantle (cloak)

The long tunic of England's Norman rulers concealed braies (flared breeches). Noblemen also wore a mantle – a simple cloak.

Japan

Junihito clothing

Getting dressed took ages in 12th-century Japan: junihitoe clothing meant "12 layers," but there could be more!

12th century Norman

Fashionable women in 12th-century France or England dressed in gowns with long hanging sleeves, and braided their hair in a long plait.

Mongolia

Long, hanging sleeve

Quilting kept the Mongol people warm. Better off Mongols (left) wore a long coat over a padded san (jacket).

13th century England

English knights swapped the long wool tunics of civilians for heavy chain mail. Ladies hid their hair and neck in a wimple.

Wimple

16th century Inca

Like the Mayans, the Inca people of Peru decorated their finest clothes with brilliant feathers. Llama wool provided warm cloaks.

England

Queen Elizabeth I loved pretty clothes. The styles she pioneered took several hours to put on.

Japan

Enormous sleeve

The kimono did not have any pockets, but its wearer could carry a handkerchief or a fan in the vast sleeves.

17th century American Puritan

The simple clothes of the Puritans showed that they rejected the richness of the Roman Catholic Church.

Arctic

The Inuit of North America kept out icy Arctic winds with furs turned ticklishly furry side in.

17th century England

In 17th-century England, lace collars and wide, plumed hats were the fashion for both sexes; men wore tall boots.

Netherlands

Ruff

The ruff, a pleated collar, grew to 24 in (60 cm) across in the 17th century, and had wire supports.

Benin

Fine kilt

The soldiers and palace guards of Benin (now Nigeria) wore fine ornamental kilts and helmets.

North America

By the late 19th century, the suit of the modern businessman had begun to emerge.

Native American people wore a variety of costumes. Ornaments showed their tribal status.

19th century England

Bustle

To simulate huge bottoms and tiny waists, fashion dictated that women wear bustles and corsets.

20th century China

Styles in the last years of Imperial China were little different from those worn centuries earlier.

1905 International

Top hat and tails, now wedding clothes, were standard dress for the office early this century.

1930s

By the 1930s, short hems had replaced long dresses, except for formal wear.

1950s

After World War II, artificial fibers made clothes cheap, comfortable, and easy to clean.

Denim

Denim, classic work fabric since the 1850s, is now considered fashionable.

MEDICINE

8000 BC Sorcerer

Headdress

Early peoples mostly relied on magicians and perhaps priests to heal their diseases and injuries with spells and incantations. The costumed figure above was painted about 10,000 years ago on a French cave wall.

6500 BC Trephining

The first known surgery was probably trephining, or drilling the skull. This may have been a cure for headache. The remains of skulls where the hole has healed suggest that some patients even survived the operation!

1600 BC Egyptian priest-doctors

Physicians of ancient Egypt knew how to set bones, how to treat a fever, and how to recognize symptoms of many curable and fatal diseases. Egyptian pharmacists dispensed powerful herbal drugs, including opium.

1500s Anatomy

Andreas Vesalius (1514-1564)

Belgian doctor Andreas Vesalius was among the first to dissect human corpses to learn anatomy (the body's structure). He proved that much of what doctors then believed about the body was untrue. In 1543 he published his findings in a book called *The Fabric of the Human Body*. As a professor of anatomy at the University of Padua, Italy, his teaching changed the course of European medicine.

1500s Paracelsus

Medieval doctors used leeches to suck a patient's blood and correct imbalances in the body.

Paracelsus (1493-1541)

Physician Theophrastus Bombastus von Hohenheim took the nickname "Paracelsus" not just because it was easier to pronounce, but to show that he rejected the teachings of Celsus and other Roman doctors ("para" means "above"). His most important idea was that the cause of disease was an agent from outside the body – what we now call bacteria – and not an imbalance within it.

1880 Vaccination

Louis Pasteur (1822-1895)

French chemist Louis Pasteur improved on Jenner's idea. He was the first to show that infecting the body with a mild form of a disease provided protection against a more severe attack of the same disease. This technique, called vaccination, now protects millions of people.

1846 Anesthetics

Before anesthetics, surgical operations were both painful and frightening. American dentist William Morton (1819-1868) was probably the first to use ether to make patients completely unconscious during surgery in 1846. He tried it first on his spaniel to see if it would work.

1865 Antiseptic surgery

Joseph Lister (1827-1912)

English surgeon Joseph Lister made surgery safer in 1865 when he began using carbolic acid as an antiseptic. He poured it on dressings and instruments to kill germs. He also sprayed it into the air of the operating theater. His technique cut infection by one-fifth.

1928 The first antibiotics

Spots of mold growing on a dish of laboratory jelly caught the eye of Scottish scientist Alexander Fleming (1881-1955). Each spot had killed surrounding bacteria. By extracting the active ingredient, called Penicillin, from the mold, Fleming isolated the first antibiotic.

1953 DNA

Francis Crick *James D. Watson*

DNA molecule

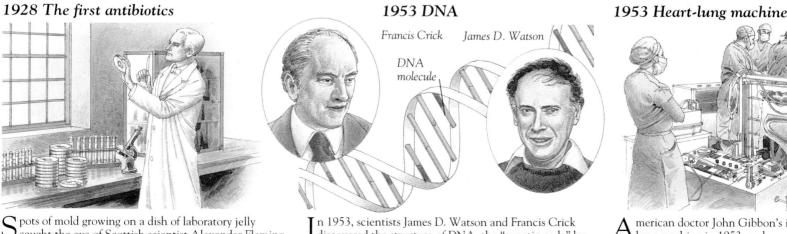

In 1953, scientists James D. Watson and Francis Crick discovered the structure of DNA, the "genetic code" by which people inherit their basic features, such as hair color, from their parents. Rosalind Franklin and Maurice H. Wilkins also provided vital clues along the way.

1953 Heart-lung machine

American doctor John Gibbon's invention of the heart-lung machine in 1953 made major heart surgery possible. The machine does the job of the heart and lungs while a surgeon operates on them. Before its invention, heart operations could not last longer than 10 minutes.

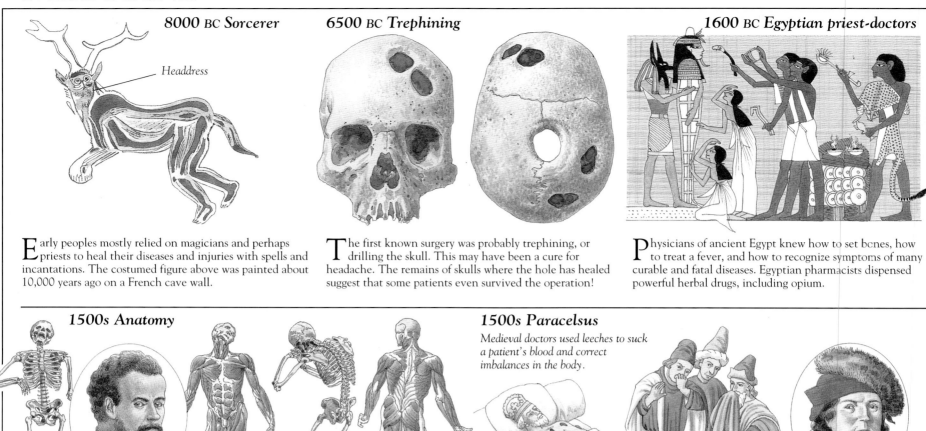

400 BC Hippocrates and Greek medicine

Hippocrates
(c. 460 BC-c. 377 BC)

Greek doctor Hippocrates was the first to separate religion from healing. He recognized the role of diet, living conditions, and climate in illness, and established a code of practice for doctors that is still in use.

500 BC-AD 400 Roman medicine

Forceps

Ladle for warming salves

Bleeding cup

Scalpel

Retractor

Scalpel handle

Hook for pulling out tissue

Medical instruments from the Roman Empire show that Roman doctors had many surgical skills. However, the Romans' major contribution to medicine was in public health – good plumbing kept Romans healthy!

Acupuncture

Since ancient times, Chinese doctors have treated patients by inserting needles into their bodies.

800s Salerno

In the Dark Ages, one of the only places where doctors could train was a school at Salerno, in Italy.

1628 Discovery of blood circulation

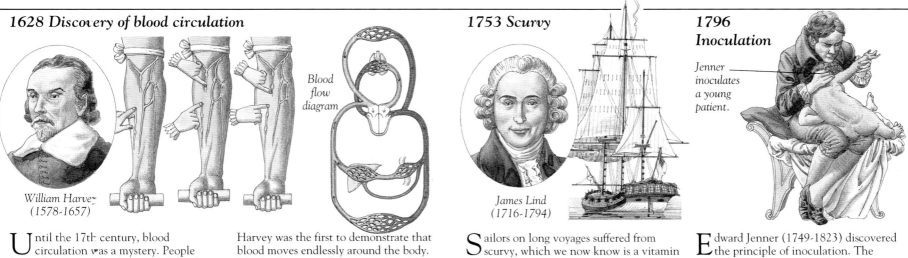

Blood flow diagram

William Harvey
(1578-1657)

Until the 17th century, blood circulation was a mystery. People knew that severe bleeding caused death, but believed that drinking blood topped up the supply. English physician William

Harvey was the first to demonstrate that blood moves endlessly around the body. Besides dissection, his 14 years' work included blocking arteries to stop the flow of blood, as in the illustration above.

1753 Scurvy

James Lind
(1716-1794)

Sailors on long voyages suffered from scurvy, which we now know is a vitamin C deficiency. Scottish physician James Lind suggested they have lime juice as a cure, giving British sailors the name "Limeys."

1796 Inoculation

Jenner inoculates a young patient.

Edward Jenner (1749-1823) discovered the principle of inoculation. The English physician protected a boy against the disease smallpox by first infecting him with cowpox – a much milder illness.

1890 Psychiatry

1896 X rays

Wilhelm Conrad Röntgen
(1845-1923)

By studying the human mind, Sigmund Freud (1856-1939) gave medicine new ways of treating mental illness. He helped patients unlock their unconscious, the hidden and troubled parts of their minds.

German physicist Wilhelm Conrad Röntgen discovered rays that he found could pass through flesh, but were stopped by bone. Röntgen rays, also known as X rays, are now an essential medical tool.

1898 Radium

Marie Curie (1867-1934) and her husband Pierre (1859-1906) studied radioactivity in Paris. In 1898 they separated the element radium. Their work led to the treatment of cancer with radioactivity.

1909 Drug synthesis

German researcher Paul Ehrlich (1854-1915) became famous for his work on immunity and drug action. He later synthesized a cure for a fatal sexually transmitted disease called syphilis.

1970s-80s CAT scanner

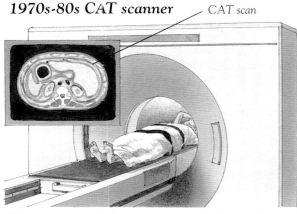

CAT scan

By scanning with X rays, doctors can build up a 3-dimensional electronic image of the body. Developed in the 1970s, computerized axial tomography (CAT) scans allow doctors to study even soft tissue, such as the brain, which would be poorly defined on ordinary X rays.

1980s-90s Microsurgery

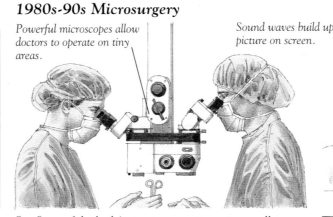

Powerful microscopes allow doctors to operate on tiny areas.

Many of the body's structures are tiny – too small to see with the naked eye. But with the aid of microscopes, surgeons can now rejoin severed nerves to restore the use of an injured limb, and carry out operations on delicate organs such as the inner ear.

1990s Ultrasound

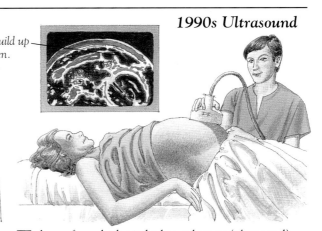

Sound waves build up picture on screen.

Echoes of very high-pitched sound waves (ultrasound) build up a computer picture of an unborn baby without exposing the child to X rays, which can cause harm. Most mothers now routinely have ultrasound scans during pregnancy to detect problems before childbirth.

Weapons

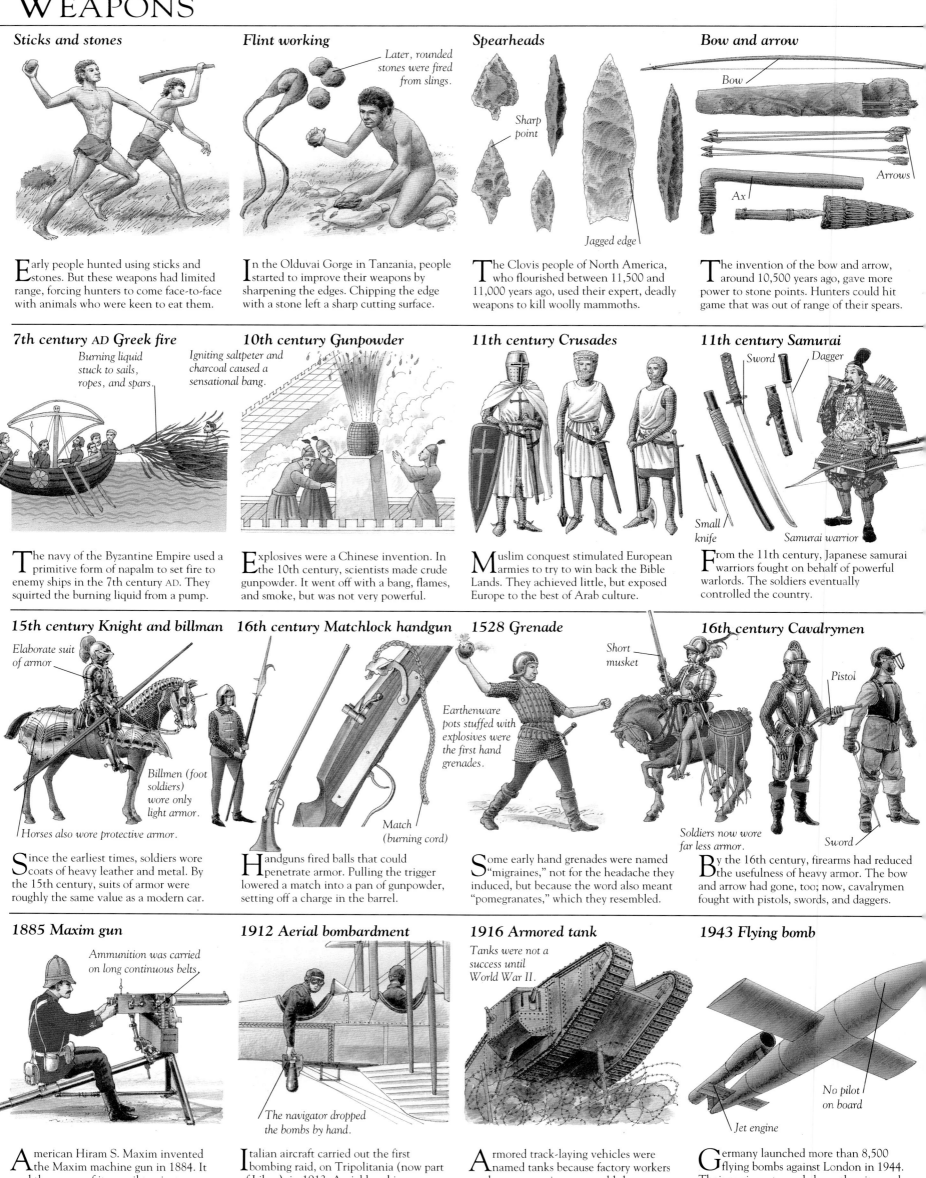

Sticks and stones

Early people hunted using sticks and stones. But these weapons had limited range, forcing hunters to come face-to-face with animals who were keen to eat them.

Flint working

Later, rounded stones were fired from slings.

In the Olduvai Gorge in Tanzania, people started to improve their weapons by sharpening the edges. Chipping the edge with a stone left a sharp cutting surface.

Spearheads

Sharp point

Jagged edge

The Clovis people of North America, who flourished between 11,500 and 11,000 years ago, used their expert, deadly weapons to kill woolly mammoths.

Bow and arrow

Bow

Arrows

Ax

The invention of the bow and arrow, around 10,500 years ago, gave more power to stone points. Hunters could hit game that was out of range of their spears.

7th century AD Greek fire

Burning liquid stuck to sails, ropes, and spars.

The navy of the Byzantine Empire used a primitive form of napalm to set fire to enemy ships in the 7th century AD. They squirted the burning liquid from a pump.

10th century Gunpowder

Igniting saltpeter and charcoal caused a sensational bang.

Explosives were a Chinese invention. In the 10th century, scientists made crude gunpowder. It went off with a bang, flames, and smoke, but was not very powerful.

11th century Crusades

Muslim conquest stimulated European armies to try to win back the Bible Lands. They achieved little, but exposed Europe to the best of Arab culture.

11th century Samurai

Sword

Dagger

Small knife

Samurai warrior

From the 11th century, Japanese samurai warriors fought on behalf of powerful warlords. The soldiers eventually controlled the country.

15th century Knight and billman

Elaborate suit of armor

Billmen (foot soldiers) wore only light armor.

Horses also wore protective armor.

Since the earliest times, soldiers wore coats of heavy leather and metal. By the 15th century, suits of armor were roughly the same value as a modern car.

16th century Matchlock handgun

Match (burning cord)

Handguns fired balls that could penetrate armor. Pulling the trigger lowered a match into a pan of gunpowder, setting off a charge in the barrel.

1528 Grenade

Earthenware pots stuffed with explosives were the first hand grenades.

Some early hand grenades were named "migraines," not for the headache they induced, but because the word also meant "pomegranates," which they resembled.

16th century Cavalrymen

Short musket

Pistol

Soldiers now wore far less armor.

Sword

By the 16th century, firearms had reduced the usefulness of heavy armor. The bow and arrow had gone, too; now, cavalrymen fought with pistols, swords, and daggers.

1885 Maxim gun

Ammunition was carried on long continuous belts.

American Hiram S. Maxim invented the Maxim machine gun in 1884. It used the power of its recoil to eject a spent cartridge and reload a new one.

1912 Aerial bombardment

The navigator dropped the bombs by hand.

Italian aircraft carried out the first bombing raid, on Tripolitania (now part of Libya), in 1912. Aerial bombing was more widely used in World War I (1914-18).

1916 Armored tank

Tanks were not a success until World War II.

Armored track-laying vehicles were named tanks because factory workers on the secret project were told they were making "water-carriers."

1943 Flying bomb

No pilot on board

Jet engine

Germany launched more than 8,500 flying bombs against London in 1944. Their engines stopped above the city, and the explosives crashed to the ground.

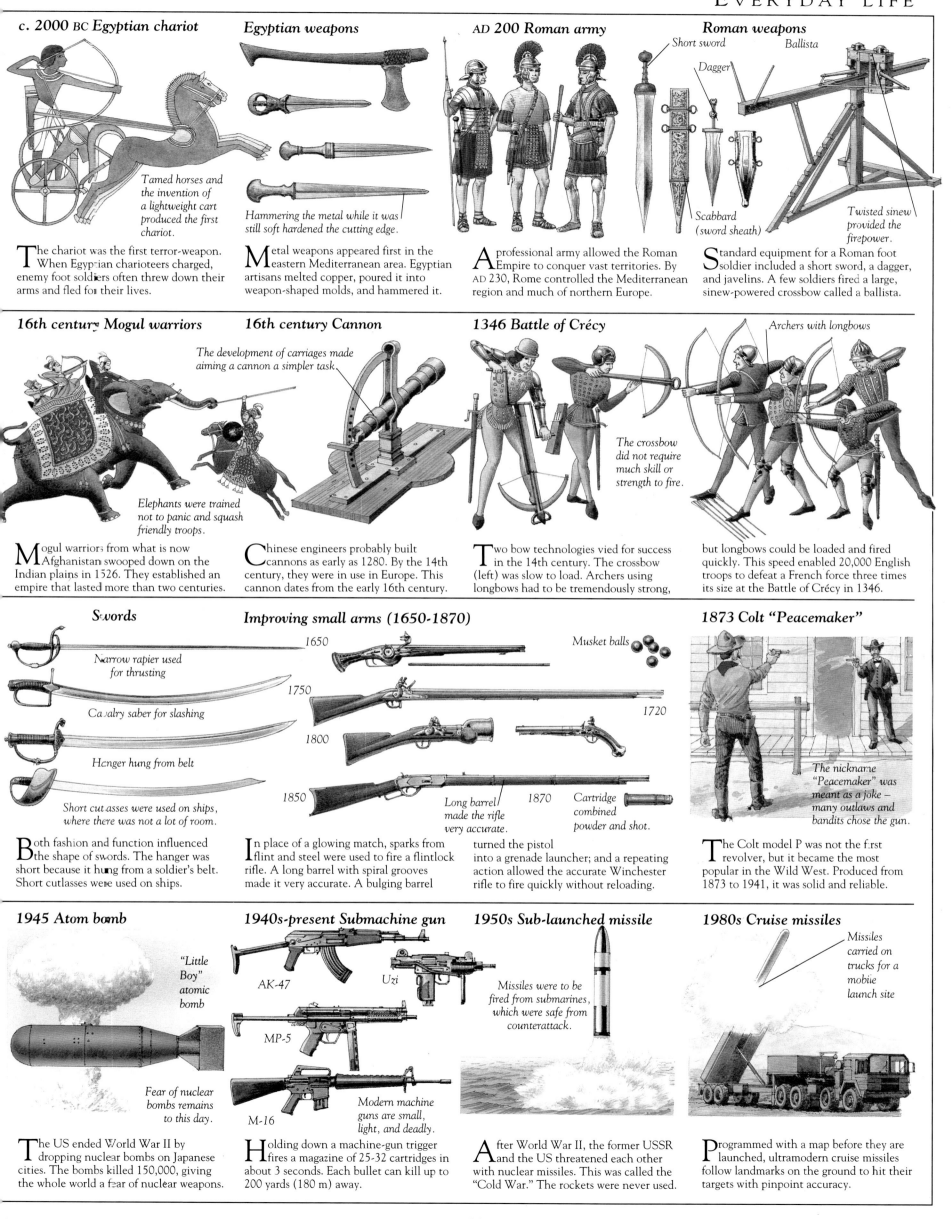

c. 2000 BC Egyptian chariot

Tamed horses and the invention of a lightweight cart produced the first chariot.

The chariot was the first terror-weapon. When Egyptian charioteers charged, enemy foot soldiers often threw down their arms and fled for their lives.

Egyptian weapons

Hammering the metal while it was still soft hardened the cutting edge.

Metal weapons appeared first in the eastern Mediterranean area. Egyptian artisans melted copper, poured it into weapon-shaped molds, and hammered it.

AD 200 Roman army

A professional army allowed the Roman Empire to conquer vast territories. By AD 230, Rome controlled the Mediterranean region and much of northern Europe.

Roman weapons

Short sword *Dagger* *Ballista*

Scabbard (sword sheath)

Twisted sinew provided the firepower.

Standard equipment for a Roman foot soldier included a short sword, a dagger, and javelins. A few soldiers fired a large, sinew-powered crossbow called a ballista.

16th century Mogul warriors

Elephants were trained not to panic and squash friendly troops.

Mogul warriors from what is now Afghanistan swooped down on the Indian plains in 1526. They established an empire that lasted more than two centuries.

16th century Cannon

The development of carriages made aiming a cannon a simpler task.

Chinese engineers probably built cannons as early as 1280. By the 14th century, they were in use in Europe. This cannon dates from the early 16th century.

1346 Battle of Crécy

Archers with longbows

The crossbow did not require much skill or strength to fire.

Two bow technologies vied for success in the 14th century. The crossbow (left) was slow to load. Archers using longbows had to be tremendously strong, but longbows could be loaded and fired quickly. This speed enabled 20,000 English troops to defeat a French force three times its size at the Battle of Crécy in 1346.

Swords

Narrow rapier used for thrusting

Cavalry saber for slashing

Hanger hung from belt

Short cutlasses were used on ships, where there was not a lot of room.

Both fashion and function influenced the shape of swords. The hanger was short because it hung from a soldier's belt. Short cutlasses were used on ships.

Improving small arms (1650-1870)

1650 *Musket balls* *1720*

1750

1800

1850 *Long barrel made the rifle very accurate.* *1870* *Cartridge combined powder and shot.*

In place of a glowing match, sparks from flint and steel were used to fire a flintlock rifle. A long barrel with spiral grooves made it very accurate. A bulging barrel turned the pistol into a grenade launcher; and a repeating action allowed the accurate Winchester rifle to fire quickly without reloading.

1873 Colt "Peacemaker"

The nickname "Peacemaker" was meant as a joke — many outlaws and bandits chose the gun.

The Colt model P was not the first revolver, but it became the most popular in the Wild West. Produced from 1873 to 1941, it was solid and reliable.

1945 Atom bomb

"Little Boy" atomic bomb

Fear of nuclear bombs remains to this day.

The US ended World War II by dropping nuclear bombs on Japanese cities. The bombs killed 150,000, giving the whole world a fear of nuclear weapons.

1940s-present Submachine gun

AK-47 *Uzi*

MP-5

M-16 *Modern machine guns are small, light, and deadly.*

Holding down a machine-gun trigger fires a magazine of 25-32 cartridges in about 3 seconds. Each bullet can kill up to 200 yards (180 m) away.

1950s Sub-launched missile

Missiles were to be fired from submarines, which were safe from counterattack.

After World War II, the former USSR and the US threatened each other with nuclear missiles. This was called the "Cold War." The rockets were never used.

1980s Cruise missiles

Missiles carried on trucks for a mobile launch site

Programmed with a map before they are launched, ultramodern cruise missiles follow landmarks on the ground to hit their targets with pinpoint accuracy.

IN THE BEGINNING ...
THE ONLY BUILDINGS WERE HOUSES. BUT AS CIVILIZATION DEVELOPED,

Parthenon, Athens

PEOPLE ATTEMPTED GRANDER CONSTRUCTIONS. THEY CREATED TEMPLES FOR WORSHIP AND BUILT MIGHTY PALACES WHERE THEIR LEADERS LIVED IN LUXURY. EQUALLY ELABORATE TOMBS HONORED THE NOBLE DEAD. AS POPULATION INCREASED, PEOPLE FOUGHT FOR FOOD, LAND, AND WATER.

To defend their own homes, they surrounded them with high walls, turning town into fortress. As travelers began to trade between towns, they found that wading through rivers slowed their progress. They began to build bridges. The story of how buildings began is fascinating.

Pyramids, Giza

20,000 YEARS AGO

EARLY PEOPLES LIVED AS NOMADS, WANDERING THE WORLD TO HUNT AND GATHER FOOD. THEY ONLY needed shelters that lasted until they moved on again. The world's population was less than a thousandth of today's levels, so battles for resources were rare and there was no need for these people to fortify their homes.

Wood-framed shelter

Celtic hall

2,000 YEARS AGO

Great Wall, China

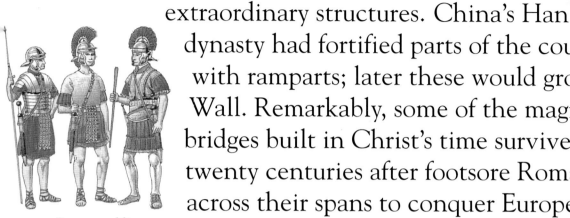

IN THE LIFETIME OF JESUS CHRIST (c.6 BC - c.AD 30), FOUNDER OF the Christian religion, the great empires of the world had already built some truly extraordinary structures. China's Han dynasty had fortified parts of the country's northern border with ramparts; later these would grow into the Great Wall. Remarkably, some of the magnificent Roman bridges built in Christ's time survive to this day, nearly twenty centuries after footsore Roman soldiers trudged across their spans to conquer Europe.

Roman soldiers

200 YEARS AGO

French aristocrats

REVOLUTIONARY FEVER GRIPPED EUROPE IN THE LATE 18TH CENTURY, AS MOB TOPPLED MONARCH IN FRANCE. Architecture, too, was changing dramatically. Advances in iron-making allowed for slender supports for new styles of bridges. This was also a time of hurried fortress building as the old empires of Europe prepared to defend themselves. The new forts resembled old-fashioned castles.

Deal Fort, England

20 YEARS AGO

ENGINEERS AND ARCHITECTS FINALLY FOUND THE MATERIALS AND TECHNIQUES THEY NEEDED TO turn age-old visions into reality in the 20th century. Skyscrapers reached the clouds. Bridges stretched to the horizon. Military builders built castles underground, hoping to resist nuclear weapons.

Sydney Opera House, Australia

GREAT BUILDINGS

2800 BC *Stonehenge*

Stonehenge faces the rising sun on the first day of summer.

We know that ancient peoples created the first grand public buildings to worship in. But the exact purpose of the shaped upright stones of Stonehenge in southern England still remains a mystery.

2500 BC *The pyramids at Giza*

Like Stonehenge, the pyramids may have had an astronomical function.

Transporting stones for just one pyramid may have taken 100,000 workers 20 years.

The Egyptian people constructed stone pyramids as tombs for their pharaohs (rulers). Tunnels in the largest align with stars that the Egyptians considered important. The most famous site is at Giza, near Cairo. Slave workers built these pyramids 4,500 years ago using vast stone building blocks weighing up to 200 tons (tonnes). They probably moved the stones to the site by barge on the nearby Nile River.

2230-2000 BC *Ziggurat at Ur*

Step pyramid, known as a ziggurat.

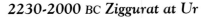

The Mesopotamian civilization, which flourished in what is now Iraq, built ziggurats. The best-known example, at Ur, was devoted to the moon god. It was part temple, part stairway to heaven.

532-537 *Hagia Sophia, Istanbul*

Minaret, or prayer tower

The Byzantine Empire continued the Roman tradition of grand buildings, but devoted them to Christian rather than pagan worship. At the church of Hagia Sophia ("divine wisdom") in Istanbul, a colossal domed roof soars over the rich interior. When the Turkish Ottoman Empire conquered the city, the church was converted to a mosque with the addition of corner minarets (prayer towers).

7th century *Horyuji Temple*

Japanese builders worked wood into light frames that were strong, flexible, and able to withstand earthquakes. Like many of the country's temples, this example from near Nara is inspired by Chinese designs.

1050 *Pueblo Bonito, Chaco Canyon*

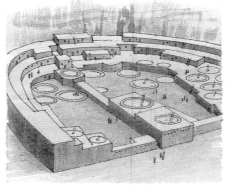

The Anasazi people who lived in Chaco Canyon, New Mexico, integrated ceremonial chambers called kivas into a remarkable D-shaped multi-story complex that also included more than 650 dwellings.

1296-1436 *Florence Cathedral*

While northern churches soared upward, in southern Europe other ways to glorify God were found. Filippo Brunelleschi (1377-1446) crowned Florence Cathedral with a vast dome. It is nicknamed *Il Duomo.*

1421 *Forbidden City, Beijing*

Architects have created some of the world's finest buildings purely for the enjoyment of wealthy or powerful patrons. At the heart of China's capital, Beijing, the courtyards of the Forbidden City were closed to all but the emperor, his family, and officials. From their construction in the 15th century until the Chinese revolution of 1911, no one else ever saw the marble halls and yellow-tiled roofs.

15th century *Machu Picchu*

Town carved out of solid rock.

Gorges on three sides hide the ruined town of Machu Picchu from the Urubamba Valley, Peru. Inca masons chose the site because it was easily defended and did not consume scarce farmland.

1675 *St. Paul's Cathedral, London*

When old St. Paul's Cathedral burned down in the Great Fire of London (1665), architect Christopher Wren (1632-1723) designed a majestic replacement in Baroque style.

1731-91 *Independence Hall, Philadelphia*

American buildings developed a home-grown style only after the country's independence. Philadelphia's Independence Hall was designed in the style known as "Georgian" after England's king of the day.

1845-7 *Kew Palm House*

Engineer Robert Turner helped design the iron-and-glass structure.

The industrial revolution made glass and iron cheap and plentiful. Architect Decimus Burton combined them brilliantly in this amazing Palm House at the Royal Botanic Gardens in Kew, near London.

1883 *Home Insurance Building, Chicago*

Cheap steel also made skyscrapers possible. William le Baron Jenney (1832-1907) built the first in Chicago, using steel as a fireproof skeleton on which to hang floors and a weatherproof skin.

717 BC Assyrian palace, Khorsabad

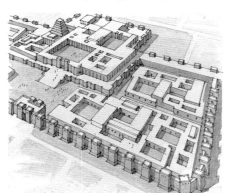

Palaces glorifying rulers soon rivaled tombs. At the palace of Khorsabad, a frieze showed soldiers building a pyramid of their enemy's heads while the king, Sargon, drove his chariot over the bodies.

447-438 BC Acropolis/Parthenon, Greece

Inside stood a 42-ft (12.8-m) gold statue of Athena with ivory skin and jeweled eyes.

The ancient Greeks crowned their cities with an acropolis, or "uppermost city." If the city was attacked, the acropolis was the last place to fall. It was always the site of a temple, and the famous Parthenon temple, at the Greek capital, Athens, was dedicated to Athena Parthenos, a warrior goddess, credited in mythology as inventor of the chariot and the trumpet. Beautiful marble statues once stood here.

AD 118-126 Pantheon, Rome

Dome 142 ft (43.2 m) across inside

Architects (building designers) of the Roman Empire became experts in the use of concrete. With it they created vast buildings like the domed Pantheon that still stands today, 19 centuries later.

1000 Zimbabwe Great Enclosure

Majestic even in ruins, the haunting palace and religious complex at Zimbabwe have given their name to the nation in which they stand. Fine granite blocks surface the tall walls and towers.

c.1000-1500 Mont St. Michel

Building rises from flat sands in Normandy, France.

Slim spires cap the fortified monastery of Mont St. Michel. Its pointed arches were the hallmark of the Gothic (old German) style that dominated European architecture from the 12th century.

1150 Borgund stave church, Sognafiord

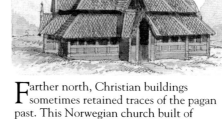

Farther north, Christian buildings sometimes retained traces of the pagan past. This Norwegian church built of staves (upright planks) has a dragon's head decoration on its roof.

c.1150-1500 York Minster

English gothic cathedrals seem to defy gravity.

With slender arches and tall spires, many English gothic cathedrals tried to defy gravity, but fell. Of those that stood, York Minster is a commanding monument to the mason's skill, strength, and ambition.

1519-47 Chateau de Chambord

Wealthy nobles of Europe have always used architecture to flaunt their wealth and taste (or lack of it). French aristocrats spent fortunes building ever grander chateaux (castles). This example from Chambord squanders space by fitting square rooms in round turrets. Unimpressed, starving French peasants destroyed many grand chateaux when revolution swept away the old order in the late 18th century.

1630-53 Taj Mahal, Agra

The tradition of the grand mausoleum (tomb) did not die with the pharaohs. Shah Jahan, Mogul emperor of India from 1628-58, built this famous monument as a last resting place for his favorite queen, Arjunand Banu Begum. Her nickname, Taj Mahal, "crown of the palace," also describes the tomb. The white marble structure makes a striking contrast with the surrounding red stone buildings of Agra.

1930 Chrysler 1954 Seagram

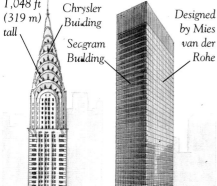

1,048 ft (319 m) tall

Chrysler Building

Seagram Building

Designed by Mies van der Rohe

Chrysler briefly had the tallest building in New York. In 1931, the Empire State Building topped it at 1,250 ft (381 m). Seagram's elegant modernist building, also in New York, has been copied many times.

1957-73 Sydney Opera House

Glass walls provide a stunning view of the harbor.

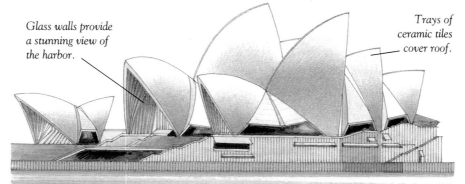

Trays of ceramic tiles cover roof.

On Sydney Harbor, the city's opera house shows that architecture can still be fun. The design by Dane Jørn Utzon (b. 1918) was chosen as the winner of an international competition held in 1956. Concrete wings echo the waves and sails on the harbor below. Computers were used to determine how the curved wings of the roof should be built. It also houses restaurants, a concert hall, library, and drama theater.

1989 La Défense, Paris

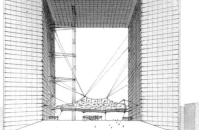

Danish architect Johan Otto von Spreckelsen created La Défense for the French defense ministry. The central opening in the 360-ft (110-m) cube is as wide as the city's famous Champs Elysées.

CASTLES AND FORTRESSES

Ditch and dike

Settlement

Ramparts (castle walls)

Fortification of Maiden Castle, in England, began in 300 BC.

Simple ditches dug around a settlement to protect it made the earliest forts. By heaping the soil they had dug alongside the ditch, the builders created a series of ramparts (castle walls) to slow attackers in their advance. People of northern Europe may have begun building these crude castles by 2000 BC or earlier.

Wooden palisade

Watchtower

Battlements

Where timber was plentiful, hilltop fortresses of upright logs were built. Reinforcing the ditches and ramparts with wood made them more difficult to climb.

Stone walls

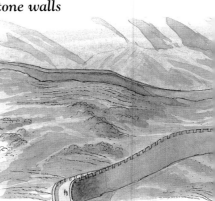

Stone fortifications are much stronger than timber and earth, and eventually all the strongest defenses were made of masonry. The Great Wall of China was

Roman siege towers

Wet animal skins stopped flaming arrows from setting the tower alight.

To scale the walls of castles they were attacking, Roman armies built siege towers. Wet animal skins protected troops in the towers from flaming arrows.

10th century Motte and bailey castle

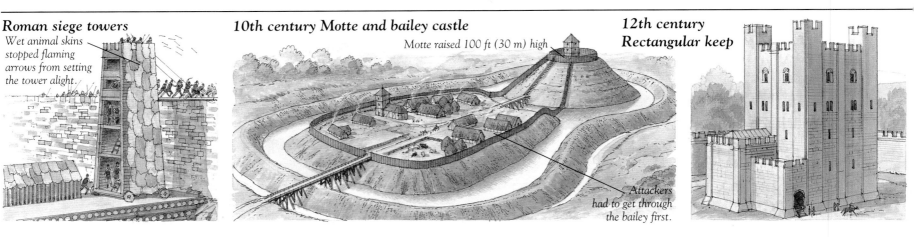

Motte raised 100 ft (30 m) high

Attackers had to get through the bailey first.

Powerful European lords began building private castles in the ninth century. Eventually these developed a characteristic design called motte and bailey. The motte (mound) was the most heavily defended area. Attackers had to conquer the baileys, or wards, before they reached the motte. In peacetime these castles lay empty.

12th century Rectangular keep

Later, a stone keep within the bailey made the castle a permanent home. The tower had a great hall above ground level, a well, a chapel, and privies (lavatories).

13th century Krak des Chevaliers

The Crusaders added an outer wall after they captured this castle from the Saracens.

The Crusaders often strengthened castles captured from their opponents. To the most famous, Krak des Chevaliers in Syria, they added an outer wall and reinforced the buildings inside. Even if attackers got past the outer wall, the new plan exposed them to merciless fire from the ramparts as they tried to storm the inner defenses.

Late 13th century Concentric castle

A strong exterior wall enclosed the outer bailey.

A second wall surrounded the inner bailey.

Toward the end of the 13th century, English castle builders abandoned the massive keep as a final defense. Instead, they designed castles on a "concentric" plan. Two walls enclosed the bailey. A large gatehouse was the center of defensive activity, and a moat (water-filled ditch) usually surrounded the castle.

16th century Blockhouse

Blockhouses were built in coastal regions.

Since they didn't contain living quarters, forts could be small and strong. Blockhouses like this one, on the coast of England, defended estuaries and bays from invaders.

1608 Himeji Castle, Japan

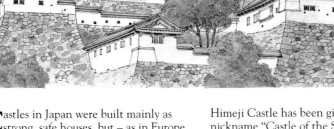

Homes for courtiers and servants surrounded the lord's home in the center.

Many Japanese castles had finely carved details and were elaborately painted.

Castles in Japan were built mainly as strong, safe houses, but – as in Europe – the size and decoration of the castle was also a measure of the owner's wealth.

Himeji Castle has been given the nickname "Castle of the Snowy Heron" because its towers are supposed to look like flying birds.

1648 Red Fort, Delhi

The massive red sandstone walls of the Red Fort, in Delhi, India, protect magnificent marble palaces. It was built for the Mogul emperor of India Shah Jahan.

Manchurian invasion

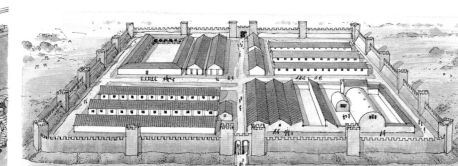

AD 120 Roman fort

among the most ambitious. Winding for 1,500 miles (2 400 km) along China's frontier with the Gobi desert, it protected against any invasion from the north.

The wall failed to keep out a Manchu invasion in 1644. Some soldiers scaled the walls, but most came in through a gate unlocked by a Chinese traitor.

Rome's highly disciplined troops built ditch-and-dike forts wherever they went, and often turned them into permanent stone-built army bases.

Solid roads marked out a rectangular plan within the walls. The forts themselves were built with comfortable barracks, a granary, workshops, and a hospital.

Late 12th century Rounded keep

Conisbrough Castle, England

The influence of the Crusades

This castle of the Counts of Flanders, in Ghent, Belgium, resembles castles built in the Holy Land during the Crusades.

A rectangular keep was convenient, but not perfect. An attacker could shelter from arrows behind the sharp corners, which were also the weakest points of the

wall. By the late 12th century, castle builders had begun to make their keeps more rounded in shape to overcome these structural disadvantages.

During the Crusades –"Holy wars" against Muslim armies – European Christian forces built, attacked, and defended many castles in the Holy Land

(now Syria and Israel). On returning to Europe, they took advantage of the lessons they had learned and built castles, such as the one above, to similar designs.

Battlements

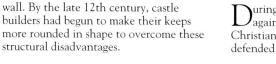

Crenel

Merlon

Shutter   *Machicolations*

On the ramparts, crenellations protected archers, who fired through merlons between them, or through machicolations, at attackers below. Shutters closed the merlons against arrows.

Bavarian castle

In Bavaria (southeast Germany), castles clung to high peaks. With their forests of turrets and towers, they have inspired the castles of fairy tales for generations.

1540 Deal Fort, England

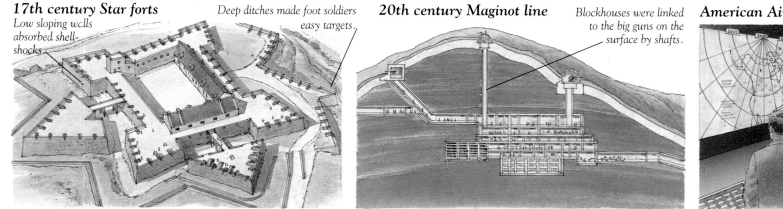

Deal Fort's low structure and curved walls deflected cannon balls.

With the development of powerful cannons, thick walls no longer guaranteed a safe home. Castles again became purely military buildings guarding

important roads, rivers, or coastlines. Deal Fort, built in 1540, is typical. The gun emplacements are open to the air so that smoke from cannons can blow away.

17th century Star forts

Low sloping walls absorbed shell-shocks.   *Deep ditches made foot soldiers easy targets.*

French military genius Sebastien le Prestre de Vauban revived interest in the castle in the 18th century with his star fort designs. Fort Ticonderoga, above, built in New York State in 1755, clearly shows the star shape for which Vauban's forts are named.

20th century Maginot line

Blockhouses were linked to the big guns on the surface by shafts.

The last great fortification was built to defend France against German attack during World War II (1939-45). The Maginot Line stretched 200 miles (322 km) from Belgium almost all the way to Switzerland. Most of the blockhouses were deep underground.

American Air Defense Command

Nuclear weapons would destroy a castle, so the US controls its missiles from a bunker under a mountain. The command center sits on springs to absorb the shock of a hit.

BRIDGES

Stepping stones | *Log crossing* | *2000 BC Clapper bridge*

The first river crossings were fords: spots where the water was shallow enough to wade (walk across). Stepping stones followed: they allowed travelers to cross without getting their feet wet.

Felling a tree over the water provided a simple way to cross even a deep river. Unfortunately, the tallest trees did not always grow conveniently close to the widest rivers. Also, balancing on a log was difficult.

Clapper bridges were first built about 3,000 years ago, using rocks piled up to form artificial islands. The gaps in between were spanned by huge, uncut stone slabs. These bridges could only cross wide, shallow rivers.

AD 100 Alcantara, Spain

Arch

Building an arch

Shaped stones of arch
Gap for final few stones and keystone
Falsework holds up the arch until it is complete.

The stone arch revolutionized bridge building. Earlier bridges required a single stone as big as the widest span, whereas an arch needs much smaller stones. Jammed together, each stone in the arch transfers the weight upon it to the next stone down. Roman engineers created magnificent arched stone bridges, such as this example from Alcantara in Spain. The bridge is nearly 20 centuries old and is still standing. It was built by Caius Julius Lacer, and his inscription on it reads: "I have built a bridge that shall remain forever."

Constructing an arch was a tricky business. Until it was complete, the arch could not stand up on its own. To take the weight during construction, the builders created a curved wooden frame, called falsework. Once the keystone at the top was in place, the arch could stand unaided.

c.1680 Drawbridge, Netherlands

Pivoting beams lift the bridge deck.

1779 Iron bridge, England

Cast iron arch

River or canal bridges must usually have arches higher than the masts of ships that sail underneath. When the masts are tall, the bridge must also be big – and costly. Moving bridges, though, cleverly solve this problem. They have roadways that swing around or lift up. This bascule, or drawbridge, was built in the 17th century and spans one of the Netherlands's many small canals.

When forges started to produce cheap cast iron at the end of the 18th century, bridge building took a giant leap forward. Cast iron was very strong compared to stone or wood. This meant the bridge supports could be small and elegant, even when the bridge was large. Englishman Abraham Darby III (1750-91) designed the world's first cast iron bridge. It had a span of more than 100 ft (30 m).

1988 Honshu-Shikoku Bridge, Japan

Suspension bridge

Today spectacular bridges carry roads and railroads across rivers and canyons that would have been impassable just a hundred years ago. Some of the world's most impressive modern bridges are in Japan, which is divided into 3,000 islands by countless seas and channels.

A chain of bridges now links the largest island, Honshu, with the island of Shikoku to the south. While none of the bridges are the largest of their kind, few bigger bridges carry both road and rail decks. The bridges cross the Seto Sea by using small islands as stepping stones: the designers built towers wherever there was land or shallow water, then linked them together. A suspension bridge carries the road and rail link south from Honshu, then concrete viaducts link this first bridge to two cable-stayed bridges that together span nearly a mile (1.5 km). The Yoshima

Wooden bridge

Logs support roadway

Rope bridge

Diagonal support ropes

A timber (cut wood) bridge is light but strong, so it can span a wider gap than either a simple log or stone bridge. The first timber bridges were quite small, like this modern example from Tibet. However, as bridge designers learned more about engineering, they created much bigger timber bridges.

Rope bridges worked on similar principles to a modern suspension bridge. All types of suspension bridges use multiple cables so that the bridge stays up even if one of the supporting cables snaps. This swaying rope bridge looks alarming, but the diagonal ropes make the bridge surprisingly stable.

c.1550 London Bridge

Heads of criminals

Shaped piers to divide waterflow

Chapel of St. Thomas

Piers rested on small, artificial islands called "starlings."

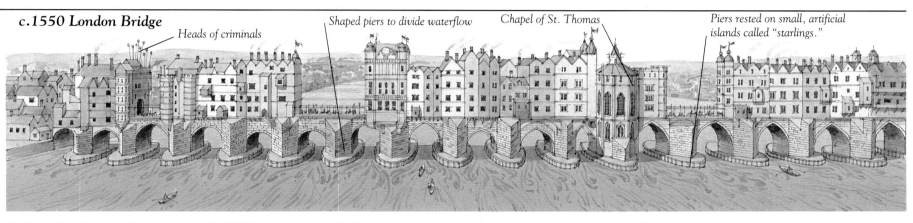

Many large European bridges built in the Middle Ages (c. AD 850-1450) supported houses, shops, and other buildings. London Bridge, built around 1180, was so packed with buildings that it formed a street. It even had a chapel in the middle, with a staff of two priests.

Heads of criminals decorated the gateways leading to the bridge. To preserve the heads after execution, they were boiled, dipped in tar, and displayed on pikes (long spears). London Bridge was very important for business, because all goods coming into the city passed over the bridge.

Wealthy medieval businessmen, grateful for the trade, often left money to "God and the Bridge" when they died, which was used for bridge maintenance. This money, invested hundreds of years ago, still pays for the upkeep of bridges in the City of London today.

1883 Brooklyn Bridge, New York

Towers anchor cables.

Steel cables support the roadway

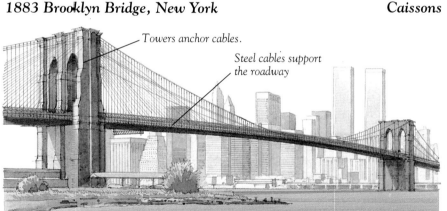

Nearly a century later, another new material – steel wire – increased the span of suspension bridges. The first person to use it was engineer John Roebling (1806-69). In 1869, work began on his Brooklyn Bridge. Its span of 1,595 ft (486 m) was bigger than anything created before.

Caissons

Compressed air line

The laborers who built the foundations of the Brooklyn Bridge worked in caissons. These were iron chambers that rested on the riverbed. Pumping compressed air into the top of each caisson forced the water out, so that the workers could dig the foundations far below water level.

1930 Salginatobel Bridge, Switzerland

Ordinary concrete is weak when used by itself in a bridge. Steel bars are very strong, and they can be used to reinforce (strengthen) the concrete and make amazing bridges. This one was built in 1930. It was designed by the brilliant engineer Robert Maillart.

Cable-stayed bridges

Suspension bridges

Viaduct

truss bridge carries the link on to a further pair of suspension bridges. Finally, a string of viaducts vaults the last 2 miles (3 km) to Shikoku. The bridges span a total of 6.2 miles (10 km) altogether, yet at top speed, high-speed trains can make the crossing in only five minutes.

Few deny that the project was a great achievement, but not everyone likes the result. Many Japanese civil engineers are conservative, and only use tested and proven construction methods. As a result, their structures can look heavy compared with those built using the newest, most advanced

technology. However, this criticism does not bother the engineers. To them reliability is far more important than an attractive shape, and as Japan is likely to achieve many more bridge-building records in the future, few can argue with their point of view.

MAKING AND MEASURING

IN THE BEGINNING . . .

I A LONG-DISTANCE CALL MEANT AN ECHOING VOICE IN A VALLEY, THE SUN PROVIDED HEAT AND LIGHT, AND THE LATEST TECHNOLOGY WAS A BETTER WAY TO FLAKE FLINT. When life was simpler and slower than it is today, communication was easy. People rarely met a stranger, and for all they knew, the world ended at the horizon. However, self-sufficiency – just a slogan now – was a matter of life and death. Without stores or markets, those who lacked the essential skills to make, mend, and build what they needed, simply perished.

Smoke signal

Talking drum

25,000 YEARS AGO

L ITTLE CHANGED IN THE FIRST 5,000 YEARS PEOPLE WALKED THE EARTH. Speech and expression were still the only way of communicating. Parents taught their children by talking to them, because no one knew how to write down knowledge and wisdom. There was a new source of energy, though: fire. Used for cooking, it made more plants edible, and fire would eventually smelt copper from rock, making sharper tools, weapons, and other implements possible. But 25,000 years ago, ancient toolmakers had not yet mastered metals. Instead, they had to be content with chipping, polishing, and sharpening stone axes and arrowheads.

Early smelting

Facial expressions

2,500 YEARS AGO

AROUND THE AEGEAN SEA, EARLY CIVILIZATION FLOURISHED. Democratic government – in which everyone made laws – began in the Greek city-state of Athens around 600 BC. Writing on parchment scrolls was by then an old way of storing information, and the Greek alphabet would eventually replace picture writing. News traveled far, but not fast: runners carried important messages. In comfortable homes, slaves cooked over charcoal.

Egyptian writing on papyrus scroll

Runner with news of the Battle of Marathon

250 YEARS AGO

IN THE 1700S, BOOKS AND NEWSPAPERS SPREAD THE WRITTEN WORD, AND THE PRINTING PRESS WAS OLD established technology. In colonial America, printer-politician Benjamin Franklin (1706-1790) watched as his newspapers were printed by hand. Steam power had not yet reached printing shops, but Franklin had a great interest in new technology. Mechanization, which was sweeping through English mills, would soon speed up American manufacturing, too.

Metal printing press, Philadelphia

25 YEARS AGO

ELECTRICITY – NOVEL IN FRANKLIN'S TIME – IS COMMONPLACE TODAY. In millions of homes electricity powers televisions showing pictures of often astonishing news events. It also provides the power for communications satellites to bounce these pictures around the world. In newspaper offices, satellites beam information in from correspondents. But in an ironic twist, power for these satellite links comes from the oldest source of all – the Sun.

Communications satellite

Cassettes, videocassette, and compact disc

THE WRITTEN WORD

10,000 BC Prehistoric art

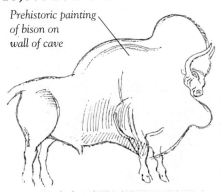

Prehistoric painting of bison on wall of cave

Written communication began with pictures. To represent a bison, early European cave dwellers sketched one on the wall. For paint, they used minerals mixed with blood, fat, or urine.

3500-3000 BC Pictograms

Paintings evolved into pictograms, like these examples from Mesopotamia (now Iraq, Syria, and Turkey). They became so abstract that they no longer resembled the objects they stood for.

Hieroglyphics

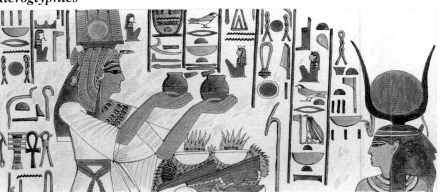

Egyptian scribes wrote in a picture-language using symbols called hieroglyphs. Other ancient cultures used hieroglyphic writing, but the characters remained in use in Egypt for longer than anywhere else: from about 3000 BC to AD 394. There were about 700 different symbols in the Egyptian system, compared to 26 in the modern alphabet. In the 19th century their meaning was discovered.

Alphabets evolving

Phoenician					
Hebrew					
Early Greek					
Classical Greek					
Etruscan					
Roman	A B C D E F G	H	I	K L M N	O P	Q R S T	V	X	Y Z

The first writing systems were very complex, with a different symbol for every object. Proper alphabets, in which each symbol instead represents a sound, began to appear between 1800 and 1200 BC. The Phoenician people, who lived in what is now Lebanon, invented the first alphabet. It had 22 letters, but no vowels. The Hebrew alphabet borrowed from the Phoenician, and the ancient Greeks based their alphabet on it 3,000 years ago. The Etruscans, and then the Romans, borrowed from the Greek to create the alphabet most widely used today.

Writing before the pencil

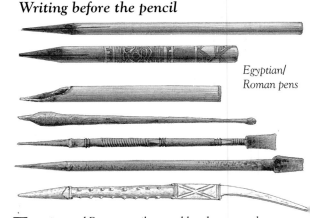

Egyptian/Roman pens

Egyptian and Roman scribes used brushes or reeds to hold and apply ink for writing. Roman writers used the tails of small animals for brushes, calling them *penicilli*, the Roman word for penis, meaning tail. This tiny brush gave its name to the modern pencil.

c.AD 1400 Madrid Codex

The Mayan civilization of Central America used hieroglyphs for writing, creating books of bark or deerskin that folded like screens. In the Madrid Codex, which survived the Spanish conquest, elaborate pictures swirl around symbols that still baffle scholars.

15th century Playing cards

The earliest use of printing in Europe was not to create books, but cards. Gambling cards came from Asia before 1377; European printers were soon printing cards from engraved wooden blocks to replace the crude hand-drawn packs used by gamblers.

1450 Printing with movable type

Johannes Gutenberg (c.1398-1468)

Printing from movable type was an Eastern invention that succeeded in Europe. German goldsmith Johannes Gutenberg was probably the first to cast individual raised metal letters, coat them in oily ink, and stamp them onto paper with a screw press.

1800-1813 Metal printing press

Printing shop c.1835

Wooden presses were only strong enough to print small pages. In the early 19th century, stronger metal presses appeared. In 1813, George Clymer of Philadelphia created the ornate Columbia Press, which used levers to squeeze paper and type together.

1837 Pitman shorthand

Isaac Pitman (1813-1897)

Taking notes at the speed of normal speech was a problem that the Romans tackled, but the first successful modern system was the invention of English schoolmaster Isaac Pitman. His 1837 shorthand system involved writing the words phonetically (by sound).

Pen improvements

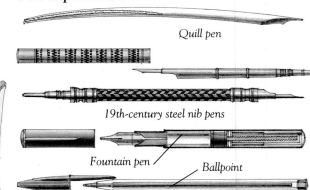

Quill pen

19th-century steel nib pens

Fountain pen

Ballpoint

Quills (goose feathers) were the standard pens from the 5th century until 1830, when steel nibs replaced them. US insurance salesman Lewis Waterman gave the pen a built-in ink supply in 1884; Hungarian Ladislao Biro's ballpoint pens replaced fountain pens in 1938.

Harvesting papyrus

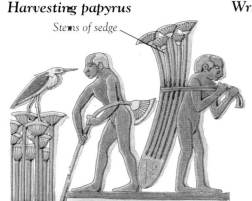

Stems of sedge

Clay tablets broke easily and took up a lot of space. From about 3500 BC, people in the eastern Mediterranean area began to make papyrus, a new writing material made from a tough, reedlike sedge (a type of grass).

Writing on papyrus

Sedge stems were beaten into sheets and rolled. Scribes wrote on them in red and black inks using brushes made of reeds. This scribe, with the head of a sacred ibis, holds a brush and palette.

3000 BC Cuneiform writing

Cuneiform writing pressed into clay slabs

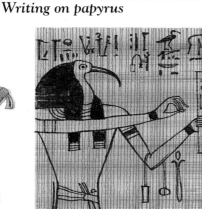

Sumerian people in Mesopotamia simplified pictograms with cuneiform writing by pressing wedge-shaped reeds into wet clay slabs. Drying the clay made the symbols permanent.

Image embossed on seal

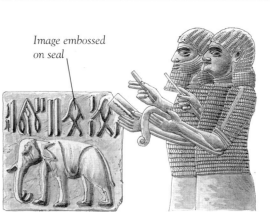

The people of the Indus Valley (now Pakistan) used seals to emboss images of their animals and gods. Nobody has yet deciphered (translated) the written characters above the pictures.

AD 105 Invention of paper

Chinese legend credits Tsai Lun (c.50-118) with the invention of paper at about AD 105. He showed that rags, tree bark, or any fibrous material could be used to make paper. The Chinese kept this a secret. Europeans still used papyrus and parchment until about 1150.

Calligraphy

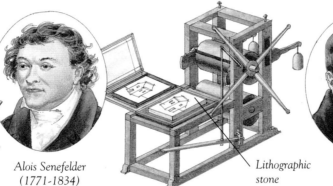

Calligraphy brush

Chinese writing has a symbol for each word, and the characters make beautiful shapes on the paper. By the 12th century, calligraphy (the skill of fine lettering) was the most respected form of art in China. Much Eastern calligraphy is written on long scrolls.

AD 868 Printed books

Like paper, printing was invented in the East. The earliest surviving printed book is the *Diamond Sutra*, printed in China in the 9th century. The printers inked engraved wooden blocks and pressed them against the paper to print the 16-ft (4.8-m) scroll.

1778-1780 James Watt's copier

Watt's copier

James Watt (1736-1819)

Though famous for his steam engines, James Watt also invented the first office copier. Not all were impressed: the Bank of England directors thought the machine would encourage forgery. In reply, Watt's angry partner described them as "hogs."

1798 Lithography

Alois Senefelder (1771-1834)

Lithographic stone

German Alois Senefelder stumbled on a new printing process in 1798 by scribbling a laundry list on a damp stone using a grease pencil. The oily printing ink stuck to the writing, but rolled off the wet areas. This process, called lithography, did not need raised letters.

1811 Steam printing

Frederick König (1774-1833)

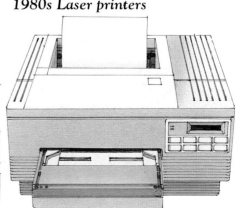

German printer Frederick König sped up printing in 1811 when he built a steam-driven press in London. His press was bought by *The Times* newspaper. Encouraged, König went on to create the "perfecting" press, which printed both sides of a page at once.

1874 Typewriter

Fast typists jammed the first typewriters. So American inventor Christopher Sholes slowed their typing. His QWERTYUIOP keyboard layout of 1874 made the most common letters the hardest to hit.

1938 Photocopier

American Chester Carlson found a way to make copies with his electrostatic copier. He became rich, but he died before revealing why photocopiers always jam when you want to use them!

1964 Word processor

The first word processors, such as this one sold by IBM in 1964, had no screens and stored text on cards, storing one page per card. Modern word processors began to appear in the 1970s.

1980s Laser printers

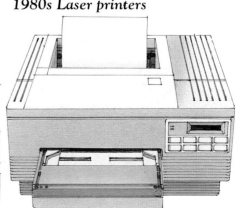

With laser printers and inexpensive desktop computers, anyone can be a publisher! These two innovations came together around 1985 to create what we now call desktop publishing.

COMMUNICATIONS AND BROADCASTING

Gestures and expressions

30 facial muscles make different expressions.

People probably learned to speak some 30- to 50,000 years ago, but they communicated with their hands and faces much earlier. Ancient peoples used gestures as expressively as any words we use today.

Drumming

Early African peoples used drums to send messages over long distances. Pitch and rhythm are very important in African languages, so drumming could express highly detailed messages very accurately.

490 BC Marathon

For longer distances, runners carried messages. Phidippides ran 26 miles 385 yds (c. 40 km) 2,500 years ago to spread news of Greek victory in the battle of Marathon. The effort killed him.

12th century AD Smoke signals

A blanket held over a fire stops smoke from rising. In still air, breaks in the smoke are visible for miles. Some early societies in the 12th century had well-established smoke-signaling networks.

1780s Sign language

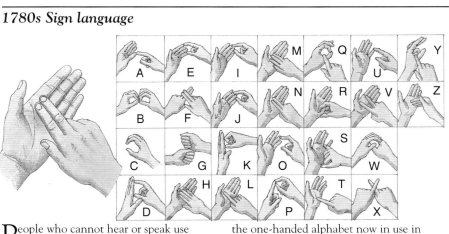

People who cannot hear or speak use hand signs to communicate. Rules in monasteries forbade talking, so monks were the first to use sign language. Frenchmen Abbé de l'Epée and Abbé Sicard developed the one-handed alphabet now in use in North America. Sicard later published a list of French words and their sign equivalents. Other countries, including Britain, use a two-handed system.

1784 Mail coach

In 15th-century England, mounted postboys carried messages, but after many complaints about their speed and drunkenness, coaches replaced them in 1784. A post-chaise (mail coach) could travel 93 miles (150 km) from London to Bath in a day; a postboy took 38 hours for the same trip. Post was expensive: charged by the mile, an eight-mile (13-km) delivery cost a laborer an entire day's wages.

1850 Pillar-box

Pillar-box in London in 1852

Fearful for their jobs, messengers disrupted the use of mailboxes in 18th-century Paris by posting mice to eat the mail inside. The first successful use of pillar-boxes was in England around 1852.

1860 Semaphore

Using just two flags, spelling out a message was quick and easy for a trained signaler. During the American Civil War, a flag system called wigwag helped troops communicate as long as they could see each other. Many navies still use flag-spelling codes like this one because – unlike radio signals – flag codes cannot be picked up by the enemy once they are out of sight of the signaling ship.

1860 Pony Express

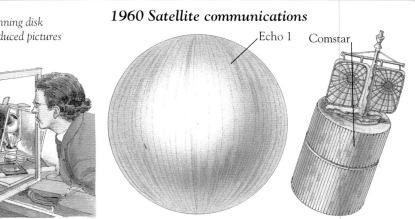

Pony riders sped American mail between Missouri and California in 1860. The Pony Express company built stables every 10 to 15 miles (16-24 km) to provide riders with a change of horses.

1896 Marconi radio

Marconi (1874-1937) started experimenting with electricity as a student in Italy.

When Italian Guglielmo Marconi was experimenting with electricity in his attic, he found that sparks created a signal he could detect from far away. Ignored by the Italian government, Marconi had to travel to England to obtain the financing to develop his invention.

1926 Baird TV

Spinning disk produced pictures

Scottish inventor John Logie Baird was the first to demonstrate a working television system in 1926, but his TV was only one of several under development at the time. It used a spinning disk to produce crude pictures and could not broadcast sound at the same time.

1960 Satellite communications

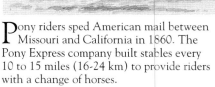

Echo 1   Comstar

The first communications satellite, *Echo 1*, was little more than a huge silver balloon. Radio waves aimed at it bounced back to the Earth. *Telstar*, which followed two years later (see page 75), relayed live television pictures across the Atlantic.

12th century Pigeon post

Message tied to leg

Trained birds can carry messages: the Sultan of mid-12th-century Baghdad, (now the capital of Iraq), was probably the first to use a pigeon post system.

1588 Beacons

A beacon can carry a yes/no message at high speed. In 1588, British people lit beacons to warn of the Spanish Armada invasion fleet. In about 18 minutes, the message had traveled across the country.

1647 Flag signals

A B C D
E F G H
I J K L
M N O P
Q R S T
U V W X
Y Z
1 2 3 4 5
6 7 8 9 10

Flapping in the breeze, groups of flags can spell out sentences. The English Navy began using alphabet flags around 1647. By the 19th century, an elaborate code cut the number of flags required: "LWV," for example, meant "Have dead rats been found on board?" Mistakes were common; a one-letter error in this signal would change its meaning to "Rash looks like red spots."

1790s Semaphore telegraph

In 1790, Frenchman Claude Chappe devised a system of sending messages that was the fastest available for the next 60 years. He built a network of telegraph towers. Each tower was in sight of two others; different positions of movable arms on the roof represented each letter of the alphabet. The tower's crew could relay messages down the line at 72 miles (115 km) a minute!

1844 Morse telegraph

Receiver for marking the tape

Dots and dashes represent each letter.

Samuel Morse (1791-1872)

Modern communication really picked up speed when Americans Samuel Morse, Joseph Henry (1797-1878), and Alfred Vail (1807-1859) invented an electric telegraph. It spelled out letters in "morse code" by switching on and off the power supply to a cable linking two telegraph stations. Morse persuaded the government to hang cables from Washington to Baltimore in 1844. Information soon flowed between the cities.

1866 Transatlantic cable

The cable-laying ship Great Eastern

Sending messages between Europe and America took 11 days until a telegraph cable, laid on the ocean floor, successfully linked the two continents in 1866. The cable was the sixth attempt in nine years; earlier transatlantic cables broke at sea, or quickly failed.

1876 Bell telephone

Scottish-born American inventor Alexander Graham Bell (1847-1922) made the first ever telephone call in 1876, when he accidentally spilled acid down the front of his pants. He shouted down the telephone for help with the words "Mr. Watson! Come here, I want you."

1891 Dial telephones

1920s "candlestick" telephone

1990s telephone

1930s telephone

Mobile telephone

All early calls were connected by an operator. In Kansas City, when callers asked for "an undertaker" they were connected to the operator's husband's funeral business. To get back his fair share of business, rival undertaker Almon B. Strowger invented the dial and automatic exchange.

1980s Fax machine

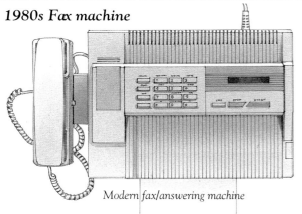

Modern fax/answering machine

Fax machines appeared in the 1980s, but facsimile transmission began more than a century ago when Italian priest Giovanni Caselli built his "Pantelegraph" in 1863. Fax machines are based on the "wire" machines that newspapers use to send their photographs worldwide.

1990s Portable satellite terminal

Journalists in remote areas find portable satellite terminals useful.

People in remote areas lacking telephone services need telephones as large as suitcases to make calls or send faxes via satellite. The planned Iridium system of 66 satellites will require only pocket-size ground stations and is intended to provide a global mobile telephone service.

1993 Videophone

Video picture

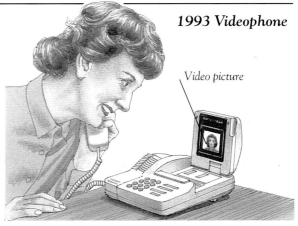

Videophones are not a new idea, but until 1993, a videophone call would have tied up 30 regular telephone lines. The first videophones sent sketchy pictures with jumpy movement, but future models will probably improve picture quality and lower the cost.

SEEING, HEARING, AND RECORDING

3500 BC Mirror

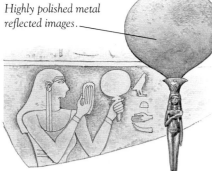

Highly polished metal reflected images.

Polished metal mirrors first appeared in Egypt about 55 centuries ago. Poor people could not afford these precious mirrors and could see their faces only by gazing into a pool of water.

4th century BC Simple lens

Greek playwright Aristophanes (c. 448 BC - c. 388 BC) knew that a lens could focus light rays. However, until the 13th century, people mainly used such lenses to concentrate candlelight on their work.

AD 800-1100 Musical notation

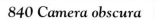

Musicians in southern India wrote the notes of their songs down as early as 700 BC. Modern musical notation, which records every detail of a tune, developed in Europe in the 8th century.

840 Camera obscura

Mirror reflects image onto glass for drawing by artist

Ninth-century Chinese writer Tuan Chêng Shih noticed that a hole in the shutters of a dark room projected a picture of the world outside. A lens and mirror were added in the 16th century.

1668 Reflecting telescope

Newton's reflecting telescope

Sir Isaac Newton (1642-1727)

In 1842 William Parsons built a reflecting telescope at his Irish castle. Its mirror was 6 ft (1.8 m) wide.

By using a saucer-shaped mirror to concentrate light, English physicist Sir Isaac Newton made dramatic improvements to the telescope. His reflecting telescopes gave a much brighter, clearer view than the refracting (lens) telescope of the time. During the following two centuries, astronomers used reflecting telescopes of increasing size to study the dimmest galaxies.

19th century Ear trumpet

Nobody knows when someone first put an animal horn to their ear and noticed that it amplified the sound, but by the 19th century, people could buy ear trumpets disguised as vases or fans.

Binaural listening device

Among many bizarre 19th-century inventions was a binaural (both ear) listening device that could also be used as a stereo speaking trumpet to amplify the human voice and send messages.

1888 Record player

Edison's wax drums wore out after a few plays, and German-American Emile Berliner (1851-1929) designed a better system of sound recording just over a decade later. From a single recording, he could make countless copies. By 1910, records had replaced the wax drums.

1898 Magnetic sound recording

Valdemar Poulsen (1869-1942)

Danish engineer Valdemar Poulsen brought sound recording into the electrical age with his Telegraphone. It recorded sound magnetically on a reel of piano wire. One of the first uses of the instrument was as a telephone answering machine.

1891 Movies

Technicolor camera

Model of Le Prince's camera

Though Frenchman Louis Aimé Augustin Le Prince patented a movie camera in 1888, he completed his work two years later. William Kennedy Laurie Dickson built the first commercially successful movie system, the Kinetoscope, for Thomas Edison in 1891-2.

1937 Radio telescope

Huge dish picked up radio signals.

American radio engineer Grote Reber (born 1911) wanted to study the radio and light signals that were sent out by distant stars. The 31-ft (9-m) dish-shaped reflector that he built in his Illinois garden to study these signals was the first radio telescope.

1947 Instant photography

Edwin Land (1909-1991)

The three-year-old daughter of American inventor Edwin Land inspired instant photography. She wanted to see a picture her father had taken as soon as the shutter clicked. In 1947 Land unveiled the process of instant photography, which produced sepia prints.

1958 Stereophonic record

Carved groove

Inventors in the 19th century developed stereophonic sound, but nearly 80 years passed before stereo records were a practical reality. The American company Audio Fidelity pressed the sound for each ear on opposite sides of a spiraling record groove.

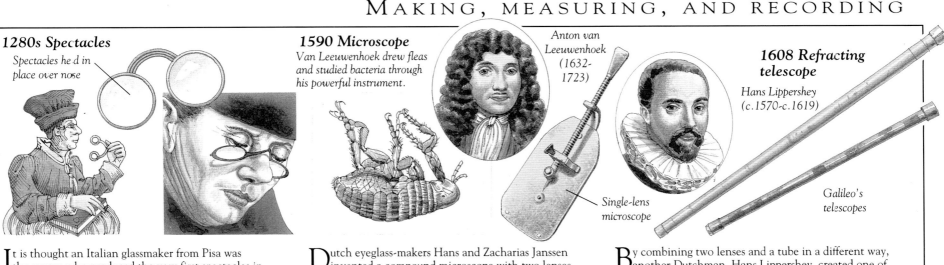

1280s Spectacles

Spectacles held in place over nose

It is thought an Italian glassmaker from Pisa was the person who produced the very first spectacles in 1286. They were originally intended as reading glasses for old people, and the Italians named them "little disks for the eyes."

1590 Microscope

Van Leeuwenhoek drew fleas and studied bacteria through his powerful instrument.

Anton van Leeuwenhoek (1632-1723)

Single-lens microscope

Dutch eyeglass-makers Hans and Zacharias Janssen invented a compound microscope with two lenses around 1590. But these instruments did not provide the high magnification of the single-lens microscopes made by Dutchman Anton van Leeuwenhoek.

1608 Refracting telescope

Hans Lippershey (c.1570-c.1619)

Galileo's telescopes

By combining two lenses and a tube in a different way, another Dutchman, Hans Lippershey, created one of the first telescopes in the early 17th century. Italian astronomer Galileo Galilei (1564-1642) used the new instrument to study the Sun and planets.

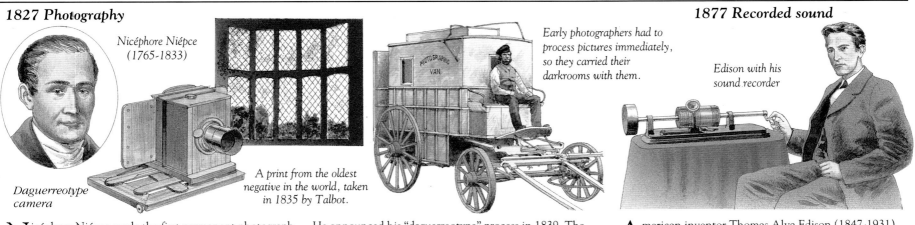

1827 Photography

Nicéphore Niépce (1765-1833)

Daguerreotype camera

A print from the oldest negative in the world, taken in 1835 by Talbot.

Early photographers had to process pictures immediately, so they carried their darkrooms with them.

Nicéphore Niépce made the first permanent photograph in France in 1827. Exposures took hours, and any movement by the subject or the camera spoiled the picture. After his death, Niépce's partner, Louis Jacques Mandé Daguerre (1737-1851), continued with the research.

He announced his "daguerreotype" process in 1839. The news astonished English inventor William Henry Fox Talbot (1800-1877) who had been simultaneously working on a similar process. The three share the credit for photography's invention and early development.

1877 Recorded sound

Edison with his sound recorder

American inventor Thomas Alva Edison (1847-1931) was the first to reproduce sound. As he turned a wax-coated drum, sound wiggled a needle pressed against it, tracing a permanent record of the sound waves. By reversing the process, Edison could recreate the sound.

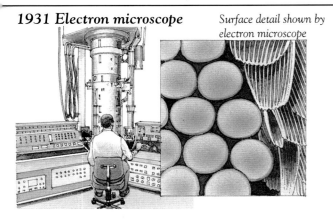

1931 Electron microscope

Surface detail shown by electron microscope

The size of light waves sets a limit to the smallest object that scientists can see using a microscope. German Ernst Ruska broke this barrier in 1931 with his electron microscope. Since 1965, scanning electron microscopes have shown objects 10,000 times thinner than this page.

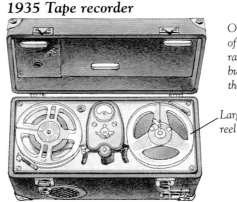

1935 Tape recorder

Large reel

Magnetic recording of sound was not a success until 1935, when the German companies AEG Telefunken and IG Farben produced magnet-coated plastic tape. Radio stations used these early machines to record the wartime speeches of Germany's political leaders.

1935 Radar

One of a chain of British radar dishes built during the war

Robert Watson-Watt (1892-1973)

Both sides in World War II (1939-1945) struggled to detect enemy aircraft using radio waves. German Rudolph Kühnhold demonstrated the reflection of radio waves by ships as early as 1933, but Robert Watson-Watt's British team was the first to develop a practical system.

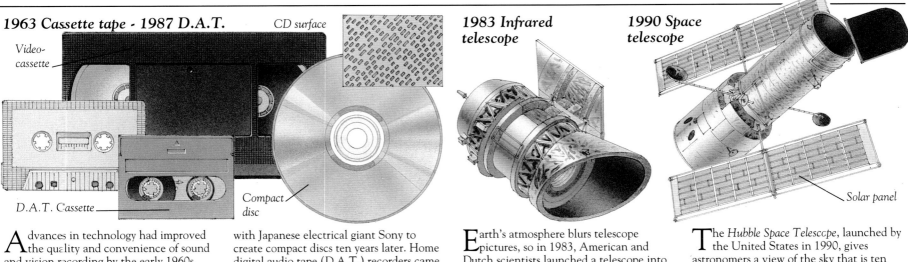

1963 Cassette tape - 1987 D.A.T.

Video-cassette

CD surface

D.A.T. Cassette

Compact disc

Advances in technology had improved the quality and convenience of sound and vision recording by the early 1960s. The Dutch company Phillips introduced audiocassettes in 1963, and cooperated with Japanese electrical giant Sony to create compact discs ten years later. Home digital audio tape (D.A.T.) recorders came out in 1987. Cassettes brought video recording home from the studio in 1973.

1983 Infrared telescope

Earth's atmosphere blurs telescope pictures, so in 1983, American and Dutch scientists launched a telescope into space. The satellite, called *IRAS*, made pictures using invisible infrared radiation.

1990 Space telescope

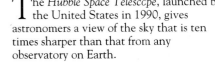

Solar panel

The *Hubble Space Telescope*, launched by the United States in 1990, gives astronomers a view of the sky that is ten times sharper than that from any observatory on Earth.

ENERGY

Sun

The Sun was the very first source of energy that people used. They basked in its heat when it shone, and shivered when it didn't, for there was no way of controlling it.

Human muscles

Human muscles at first provided the only motive (moving) power, and for nearly 1.6 million years there was no better way of moving things around. Rollers helped move very heavy loads.

500,000 years ago Fire

Lightning strikes gave early humans a first glimpse of fire. Chinese people from the Beijing area learned how to control and manage this energy source half a million years ago.

3000 BC Animal power

Farmers in the eastern Mediterranean area first began to harness oxen to simple plows 5,000 years ago. They may have packed loads onto the backs of oxen and other animals at an earlier date.

300 BC Water power

Mill wheels probably originated in mountainous regions of the Near East.

The first water wheels were inefficient. Spinning horizontally, they needed a fast-flowing stream. They could only provide enough power to grind flour to supply the needs of just one family.

1st century BC Vitruvian mill

Roman mill near Arles, France

Mill wheels that turned vertically made better use of slow-flowing water. They are sometimes called Vitruvian mills after their inventor, Roman architect Marcus Vitruvius Pollio (flourished 46-30 BC).

AD 650 Windmill

The earliest windmills turned on a vertical axis, grinding corn in 7th-century Iran and Afghanistan. European windmills, with sails on a horizontal wind shaft, were likely a 12th-century invention.

1709 Coke

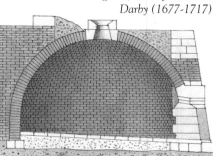

Domed ovens in Shropshire, England, built by Abraham Darby (1677-1717)

English ironworkers started to use coke as a fuel when a shortage of wood made charcoal expensive in the 18th century. They made coke by heating coal in brick ovens to drive out impurities.

1881 Hydroelectric power

Vast dams like this one turned hydroelectricity from a novelty into a practical source of power.

The first electricity supplies came from generators powered by steam engines. Hydroelectric power, produced by directing river water through turbines, came later. One of the first hydropower plants was in operation in 1881 at an old leather mill at Godalming, England.

1904 Geothermal energy

Systematic use of heat from the Earth's crust started in 1904 when a plant at Larderello, Italy, began generating electricity from fumaroles (volcanic holes emitting steam). Geothermal power supplies a third of El Salvador's electricity and water from hot springs heats most Icelandic homes.

1942 Nuclear power

Italian-American physicist Enrico Fermi (1901-1954) was the first to demonstrate that nuclear energy was potentially a source of limitless nonpolluting power. He built his "atomic pile" shown above – the forerunner of a nuclear reactor – in 1942. Thirteen years later a reactor at

1975 Bio-fuels

Filling a car with ethanol

Spirit lamps have long used distilled alcohol as a fuel, but large scale use of bio-fuels began only in the 1970s when oil prices rose. Brazil led the way with its Proalcohol program, which started in 1975.

A third of Brazil's cars now run on ethanol produced from sugarcane. Though bio-fuels cut pollution, critics point out that cultivating, harvesting, and processing the cane crop uses as much fuel as it produces.

1982 Wind power

Newest turbines have rotors 328 ft (100 m) in diameter.

Modern exploitation of wind power began in 1982 at Columbia River Gorge, in Washington State, with a three-turbine wind farm producing 2.5 mw (enough power for 2,500 homes). Now

common, wind farms are no more popular than other power sources. Masts are ugly and noisy, and to generate enough power for a city, a wind farm covering 20-40 percent of the city area is needed.

Dung

Burning dung starves the soil of valuable nutrients that aid crop growth.

In treeless regions, people set fire to animal dung and bones. Even today, dung fires still provide much of the energy for heating and cooking in rural areas of less developed nations.

3000 BC Charcoal

Covering burning wood excludes air, turning the wood into charcoal. Charcoal burns without smoke, making it a cleaner heat source. Egyptian glassmakers used charcoal furnaces around 3000 BC.

Before 1100 BC Coal

Coal burning began in China or India more than 3,000 years ago. At first, outcrops of the "black ash" on the surface were the only source, but underground mines began in the 18th century.

Tallow and other animal oils

Animal oils, fats, and greases, such as tallow, have provided energy since ancient times. The Inuit used whale blubber oil long before commercial whaling began off the coast of Spain in the 12th century.

1712 Steam power

An English ironmonger, Thomas Newcomen, (1663-1729) was the first to harness the power of steam. He used his "atmospheric engine" to pump water from mines near his home in southwest England.

1815 Coal gas

Simply heating coal generates a burnable gas. Difficulties with collecting and distributing this coal gas delayed its use until 1815. At first it smelled so foul it was only suitable for outside street lighting.

1859 Mineral oil

Drake and his oil well

Derricks quickly crowded the landscape on oil fields.

Chinese scholars in the 11th century knew that mineral oil was a useful fuel. One wrote "its smoke, which is very thick, makes the curtains all black." However, large-scale commercial exploitation of oil did not begin until 1859 when American Edwin L. Drake (1819-1880) drilled an oil well in Titusville, Pennsylvania. In the next 40 years, US oil production rose to 60 million barrels a year.

Nuclear power plant

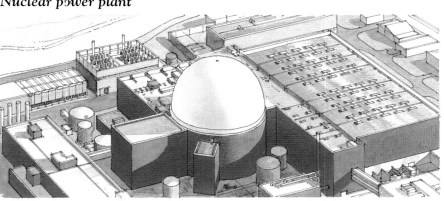

Obninsk, near Moscow, began to generate electricity in commercial quantities. Nuclear reactors supply seven out of every ten houses in France with electricity, but many nations have stopped building nuclear power plants because of safety fears. One of the worst accidents occurred in 1986 at Chernobyl, in the then Soviet Union. Large amounts of radioactive material were released into the atmosphere.

1945 Offshore gas fields

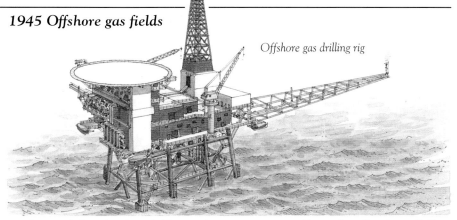

Offshore gas drilling rig

The search for oil and gas fields spread to the seabed in 1945 with a well off the coast of Louisiana. Like oil, gas is usually piped ashore from a drilling rig. The oil industry once regarded gas as a nuisance, and burned it off at the well. By 1870, though, its value was recognized. Gas was first collected at Bloomfield, New York – a pipeline made of drilled pine logs transported the fuel 25 miles (40 km).

Wave and tide power

Nodding duck generator used to harness wave power

Wave power is difficult to harness, but dams across river estuaries have been extracting energy from the tides since 1966. Generators such as this nodding duck are still at the experimental stage.

Solar heating

Hot water supply flows through roof and wall panels to collect Sun's heat.

The simplest form of a solar (sun) energy collector is a flat panel. The panels can contribute to household energy requirements even when outdoor temperatures are as low as 50°F (10°C).

Photovoltaic cells

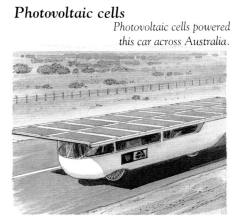

Photovoltaic cells powered this car across Australia.

Solar cells generate power directly from the Sun and have been used since 1955. They are costly and work only in direct sunlight. Newly developed cells may be "the cheapest source of energy known."

Fusion reactor

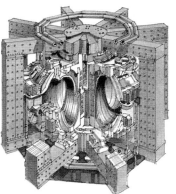

Forcing atoms together at extremely high temperatures, scientists hope one day to create power using the same processes as the Sun. Magnets surrounding the reactor prevent gases inside from touching the walls.

INDUSTRY

c. 400,000 BC *Stone tools*

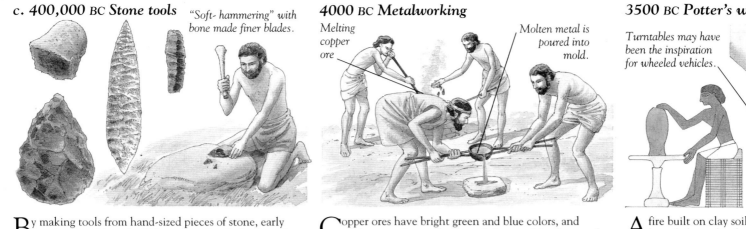

"Soft- hammering" with bone made finer blades.

By making tools from hand-sized pieces of stone, early people were able to build homes, make clothing, and prepare food more easily. At first they simply bashed the stones to create crude cutting edges, but by about 8000 BC people made finely sharpened stone axes and blades.

4000 BC *Metalworking*

Melting copper ore

Molten metal is poured into mold.

Copper ores have bright green and blue colors, and ancient people may have used the metal for face- and body-painting before they realized its potential for tools. Copper casting began about 6,000 years ago in what is now Iran: tin was added 5 centuries later to produce bronze.

3500 BC *Potter's wheel*

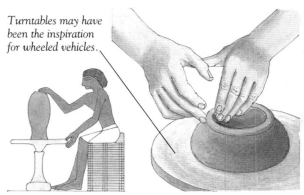

Turntables may have been the inspiration for wheeled vehicles.

A fire built on clay soil hardens the hearth: using this knowledge to harden a child's mud pie possibly led to the first pots. Mesopotamian potters were probably the first to shape their work on a turntable, from about 3500 BC. Turntables may have inspired wheeled vehicles.

AD 1000 *Spinning wheel*

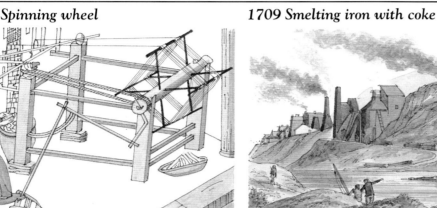

Chinese workers devised the forerunner of the spinning wheel 1,000 years ago to reel silk fibers from cocoons spun by moths. When European textile workers began using the new spinning technology three centuries later, it doubled their output of fabric.

1709 *Smelting iron with coke*

Until the 18th century, scarce charcoal fueled virtually all iron-smelting furnaces. But around 1709, English ironworker Abraham Darby I (1678-1717) found a way of making cast iron using plentiful coke (purified coal). His innovation aided growth in the manufacturing industry.

1769 *Waterpowered spinning*

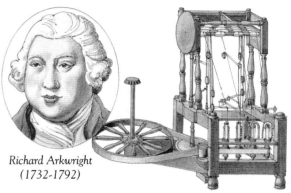

Richard Arkwright (1732-1792)

Applying water- (and later steam) power to what was formerly handwork also helped boost production. The fabric industry led the way: Richard Arkwright invented waterpowered spinning machines and gathered spinners to work them in his pioneering English factory.

1801 *Silk weaving*

Modern computer-controlled machinery had its origins in a textile factory where French weaver J.M. Jacquard devised a loom controlled by punched cards. His loom could create intricate and beautiful patterns at high speed and without errors – all under automatic control.

1818 *Copying lathe*

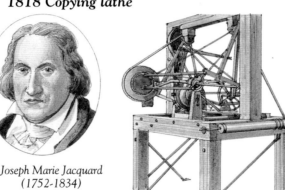

Joseph Marie Jacquard (1752-1834)

Massachusetts inventor Thomas Blanchard (1788-1864) invented his copying lathe to mass-produce rifle stocks. The operator moved a pointer over a model of the stock, and a cutter pressed against a fresh piece of wood and traced the outline of the original.

1829 *Sewing machine*

Fearing unemployment, tailors smashed Thimonnier's workshop.

Singer sewing machine

The first sewing machines were the invention of French tailor Barthélemy Thimonnier (1793-1859), but US inventors perfected the idea, turning it from a novelty into a practical device. The Singer sewing machine, a home version, was the first labor-saving household appliance.

1913 *Assembly line*

American engineer Henry Ford (1863-1947) pioneered the assembly line. A conveyor belt moved cars past a line of workers, each of whom added a new part. With the aid of standardized parts, the assembly line made cars much cheaper. By 1920, every other car on the road was a Ford.

1914 *Time-and-motion study*

Frank and Lillian Gilbreth studied efficiency. They found that a stoker worked best with a 21-lb (9.5-kg) shovel. Bigger shovels were too heavy to swing easily; smaller ones held less coal.

1950s *Automatic turret lathes*

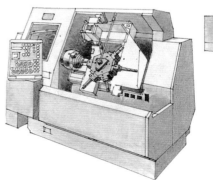

Machine tools that did different jobs on a piece of metal were invented in the 19th century. In the next century, tool changing was automatic, giving operators "set and forget" convenience.

1960s *Numerical control*

Numerical control completes the automation of machining operations: a code of holes punched in paper tape controls all the machine's processes.

2500 BC *Drilling machines*

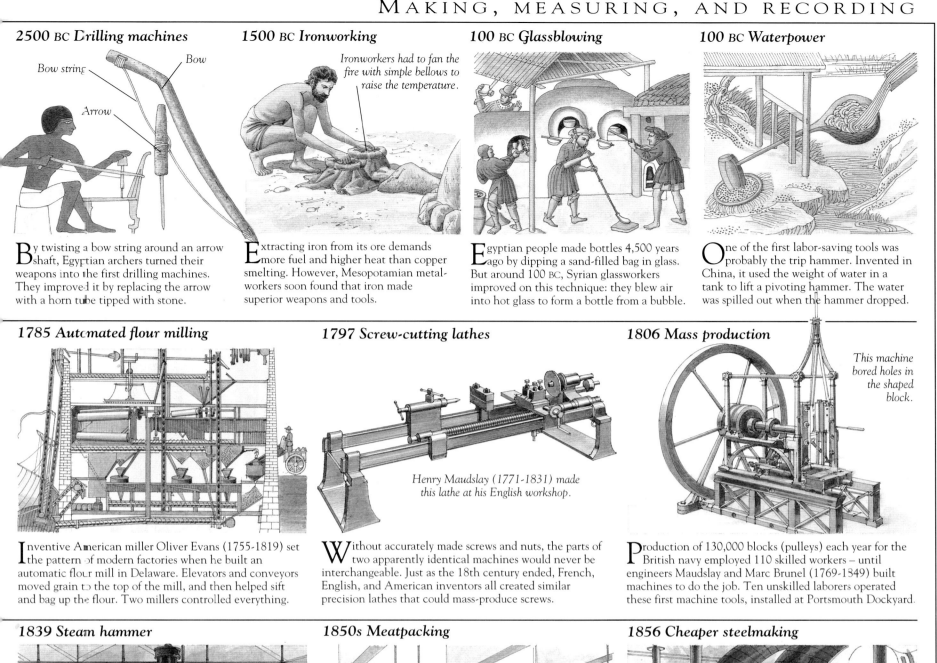

Bow string

Bow

Arrow

By twisting a bow string around an arrow shaft, Egyptian archers turned their weapons into the first drilling machines. They improved it by replacing the arrow with a horn tube tipped with stone.

1500 BC *Ironworking*

Ironworkers had to fan the fire with simple bellows to raise the temperature.

Extracting iron from its ore demands more fuel and higher heat than copper smelting. However, Mesopotamian metalworkers soon found that iron made superior weapons and tools.

100 BC *Glassblowing*

Egyptian people made bottles 4,500 years ago by dipping a sand-filled bag in glass. But around 100 BC, Syrian glassworkers improved on this technique: they blew air into hot glass to form a bottle from a bubble.

100 BC *Waterpower*

One of the first labor-saving tools was probably the trip hammer. Invented in China, it used the weight of water in a tank to lift a pivoting hammer. The water was spilled out when the hammer dropped.

1785 *Automated flour milling*

Inventive American miller Oliver Evans (1755-1819) set the pattern of modern factories when he built an automatic flour mill in Delaware. Elevators and conveyors moved grain to the top of the mill, and then helped sift and bag up the flour. Two millers controlled everything.

1797 *Screw-cutting lathes*

Henry Maudslay (1771-1831) made this lathe at his English workshop.

Without accurately made screws and nuts, the parts of two apparently identical machines would never be interchangeable. Just as the 18th century ended, French, English, and American inventors all created similar precision lathes that could mass-produce screws.

1806 *Mass production*

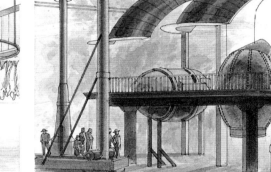

This machine bored holes in the shaped block.

Production of 130,000 blocks (pulleys) each year for the British navy employed 110 skilled workers – until engineers Maudslay and Marc Brunel (1769-1849) built machines to do the job. Ten unskilled laborers operated these first machine tools, installed at Portsmouth Dockyard.

1839 *Steam hammer*

In 1839 English engineer James Nasmyth (1808-1890) applied steam power to shape metal. His powerful steam hammer forged huge paddle-wheel shafts for a ship, but it crunched down with precision: "it can be graduated as to descend with power only sufficient to break an eggshell."

1850s *Meatpacking*

By the mid 19th century, meatpacking in parts of the US had become a city industry. Pig butchers in "Porkopolis" (Cincinnati) boasted that they wasted nothing but the squeal. In the packing factories, an overhead conveyor system was one of the forerunners of the assembly line.

1856 *Cheaper steelmaking*

British industrialist Henry Bessemer (1813-1898) called his steelmaking process "The Manufacture of Iron without Fuel." He pumped air through the molten metal; this burned off the unwanted carbon, further heating the steel. Bessemer made steel cheaper and more plentiful.

1980s *Computer-aided design*

Ever more powerful computers developed in the 1980s extended automation into the design studio. Engineers can now visualize the shape of components on screen (computer-aided design, or CAD) and use the same computer data to control the manufacturing process.

1980s *Robot manufacturing*

Engineers once had a vision of the "lights out" factory: lighting wouldn't be needed because robots would do all the work. However, unlike humans, robots are not adaptable, and can't cope when things go wrong. In the future, robots will probably only do repetitive tasks.

1990s *Microengineering*

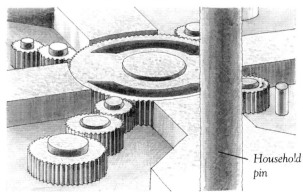

Household pin

Microengineering can create microscopic components. Tiny sensors built using this technique trigger the inflation of airbags in cars, and one day microengineers hope to make remote-controlled medical robots small enough to swim through your veins and carry out surgery.

TRANSPORTATION

IN THE BEGINNING ...

A JOURNEY MEANT TWO THINGS, BOTH OF THEM FEET. CHILDREN AND A LUCKY FEW ADULTS SOMETIMES MANAGED TO HITCH A RIDE, BUT BASICALLY WALKING WAS THE ONLY FORM OF TRANSPORTATION.

Roman ox-powered ship

Taming the ox, ass, horse, and camel broadened the choice, but the invention of the wheel really got transportation rolling. Today, rapid transit is commonplace, and we casually buy an airline ticket. It's easy to forget that in the past, speedy travel meant something different.

Early horse transportation

10,000 YEARS AGO

THE WORLD'S FIRST EXPLORERS COULD TRAVEL NO FASTER THAN THEY COULD RUN, AND THE SPEED OF COLONIZATION WAS EVEN SLOWER. By 8000 BC the first families had reached the southernmost tip of South America, 30,000 years after their ancestors first set foot on the North American continent. Without wheels or pack animals, these communities had spread south from what is now Alaska, moving about 550 yards (500 m) each year. Transportation on water was just developing: on the sheltered Aegean Sea, fisherfolk built the first boats. They poled and paddled their crude vessels – there were no sails yet.

Early sailing ships came later

Early wheelbarrow

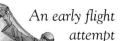
An early flight attempt

1,000 YEARS AGO

BY AD 800, THE FASTEST FORM OF TRAVEL WAS BY SEA, AND THE VIKING PEOPLE OF Scandinavia used the sea to raid Europe in longboats, traveling at a heady 10 or 11 knots (13 miles/20 km an hour). On horseback, messengers warning of the attacks managed half that speed. In England, a 15-year-old trainee monk strapped wings to his arms and tried to travel even faster – flying.

Norman ship, 1066

Bicycle, c.1890

100 YEARS AGO

THINGS WERE MOVING A LOT MORE QUICKLY BY THE 1800S. Steam trains held records reaching 90 mph (144 km/h). On roads, bicycles provided mobility for people too poor to own horses. Cars – soon to become a universal means of transportation – were slow, noisy, and terrifying for the horses that dominated traffic. At sea, steamships ferried European emigrants to North America, crossing the Atlantic in six days. In the air, balloon ascents drew crowds, and true powered flight was less than a decade away.

Early balloon ascent

10 YEARS AGO

ASTRONAUTS WERE REGULARLY CIRCLING THE WORLD IN TWO HOURS BY THE 1980S. Few people noticed. Things had been different when space travel started 25 years earlier. The "Space Race" between the United States and Russia to land the first man on the Moon had made news headlines around the world. Now, human-powered flight, first achieved in 1977, has captured the world's imagination, reawakening an age-old dream.

Astronaut

Modern helicopter

MUSCLE POWER

Shouldering the burden

As soon as humans learned to walk upright, they discovered transportation problems. Carrying even small weights slowed travelers, and heavy loads limited the distance they could move each day.

Pole and bearers

Slinging an awkward load from a pole enabled two people to carry it more easily. Between them, they could move more than twice the weight that each could carry alone.

Tump line

Other simple devices helped ease the burden of transportation. The tump line – a load-carrying strap passing over the forehead – allowed people to lift and carry more than their own weight.

Sled

Made of animal skin or bark, sleds slid easily along the ground, even when heavily loaded. Today we associate sleds with snow, but early people also used them on grass and marshland.

2000 BC War chariot

Mesopotamian warriors equipped their chariots with lightweight spoked wheels and harnessed them to pairs of galloping horses. The result was a fast, terrifying war machine.

1400 BC Mouth bridle

A harness put less pressure on the horse's windpipe than a yoke, so it could pull harder.

Mouth bridle

Onager and oxen drivers controlled their animals with a bridle that passed through rings in the beast's nose or lip. For horses, though, a mouth bit provided greater control.

Camels

The one-humped dromedary was a useful source of milk, leather, and wool.

The camel's ability to survive in the desert made it a natural species for domestication on the Mediterranean's eastern and southern shores. Both species of camel, the one-humped dromedary and the two-humped bactrian camel, were domesticated by 1500 BC. The Roman army employed camels for desert warfare.

14th century Long-wagon

Wickerwork supported the canvas cover at first, but later, hoops were used.

16th century Coach

The leather straps were the origin of the word "suspension."

Only nobility could afford to travel by coach because pulling the heavy vehicle required the muscles of a team of costly horses.

The first passenger vehicles were simple farm carts. However, by the 14th century, wagonwrights (wagon builders) had begun to create vehicles to move people in a little more comfort.

The long-wagon provided a very bumpy ride on rutted, muddy roads. But by the 16th century, cartwrights had taken steps to improve the comfort of travelers. They made the wheels and frame first, then suspended the body of the wagon by straps or chains, which cushioned the bumps. Germans called this vehicle a *kutsche*, which was the origin of the English name, coach. Bad roads still made journeys outside towns very eventful. Travelers took servants with ropes and logs to move the coach if it got stuck. Some potholes were vast. In 1571, a German farmworker fell to his death down a pothole near Frankfurt.

1838 Brougham

1840s Concord stagecoach

Private coaches in the 19th century were still heavy and required several horses, so English gentleman Henry Brougham (1778-1868) devised a small, lightweight coach that a single horse could pull. The first "broughams" had bodies just 4 ft (1.2 m) long and seated two passengers. Later models had an extra seat. The brougham quickly became popular, especially with doctors on their rounds.

The classic stagecoach that dominated long distance North American travel before the arrival of the steam train took its name from Concord, New Hampshire. There, Lewis Downing built the first examples. Pulled by a team of four or six horses, the Concord coach carried the mail. In addition, nine passengers could ride inside, and as many more were able to cling to the roof and sides.

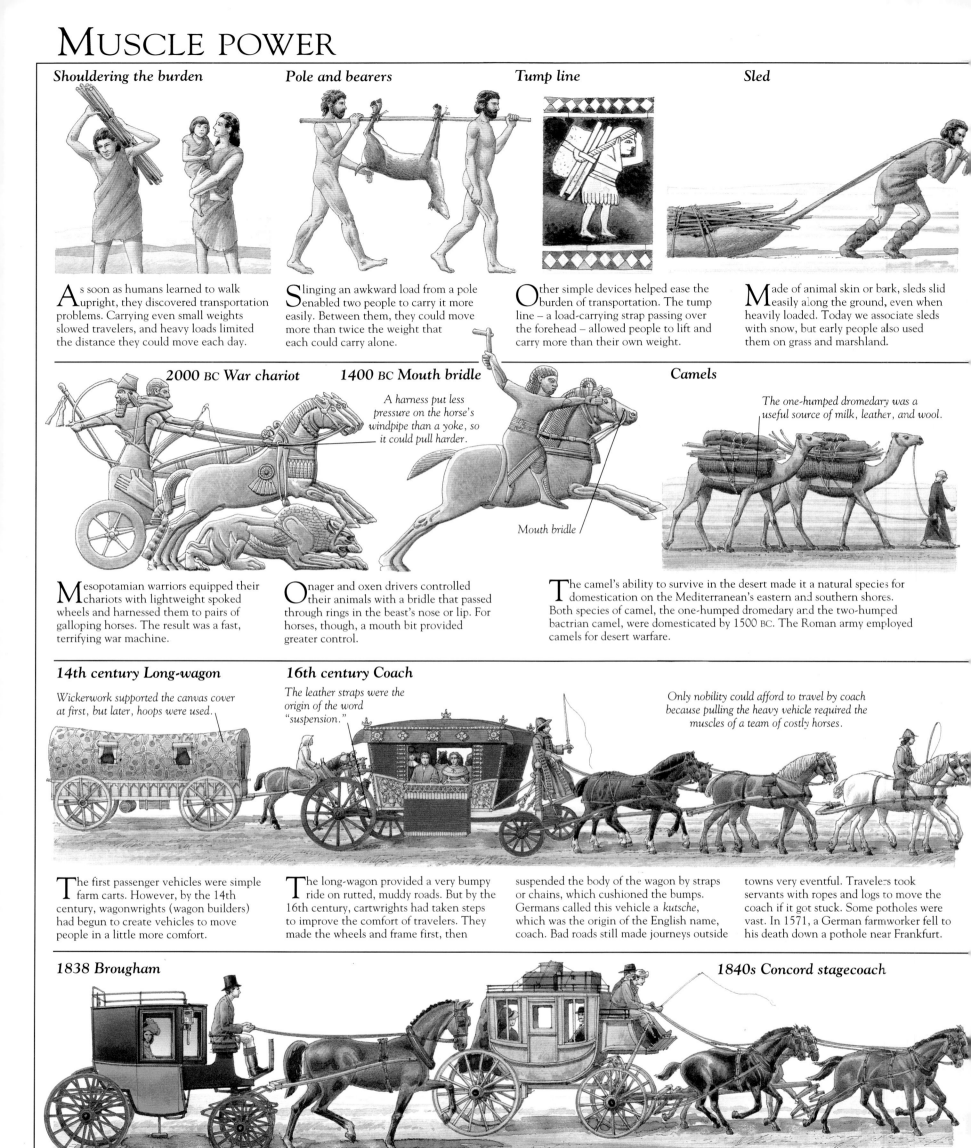

4500 BC Pack horse

Onagers and asses were used before horses.

3500 BC Cart

5000-1000 BC Travois

A dog could easily pull a quarter of a bison carcass on a travois.

When people domesticated animals, they soon realized that the beasts' broad backs could carry heavy weights. The ass was the first beast of burden, carrying loads in Egypt 7,000 years ago.

Wheeled vehicles first came into use in Mesopotamia (an ancient civilization in what is today called Iraq). The solid wheels resembled potter's turntables, which were an earlier invention.

However, no one knows who had the bright idea of fixing pairs of turntables to a rigid sled and hitching it up with a primitive harness to a couple of onagers (horselike animals).

Native North American people used dogs to drag their tepees. From this they may have developed the travois – a sled that slid on pole ends. Horses, introduced by Europeans, increased the carrying capacity.

200 BC Saddle and stirrups

AD 230 Wheelbarrow

The Chinese barrow had a huge wheel and was often sail-assisted.

3rd-7th century Padded horse collar

Rigid, padded horse collar

The first horse riders probably sat on a blanket thrown over the horse's back, but this was a precarious seat. Chinese horsemen developed a more stable saddle around 200 BC. Around the same time, horsemen in India developed a simple stirrup.

Another Chinese invention, the wheelbarrow, sped up construction work. The stretcher it replaced required someone to lift each end – whereas a wheelbarrow needs just one person pushing.

A throat and girth harness compresses the windpipe of a horse, cutting the load it can pull. From about the third century, Chinese farmers solved this problem by hitching their wagons to a rigid, comfortable padded horse collar. This simple innovation allowed the horse to pull four times the load.

18th century Stagecoach

18th century Conestoga wagon

The first public coach services began in the mid 17th century. The coaches traveled in stages, and coachmen changed the horses at the end of each stage.

This practice gave the stagecoach its name. Carrying mail, the coach traveled "post-haste," but this was hardly fast: covering 15 miles (25 km) a day was considered a good speed in the 1650s.

The descendants of European colonists headed west to the American frontier in Conestoga wagons. These distinctive vehicles had curved floors and high sides to stop their loads from shifting, and broad

wheels to spread the weight. Pulled by a team of oxen or horses, they could carry up to six tons (tonnes). Conestoga wagons took their name from a region in Pennsylvania where wagonwrights first built them.

19th century London Omnibus

"Omnibus" means "everyone" in Latin.

1832 Streetcar

OAKEY'S KNIFE POLISH

CITY & GLOUCESTER TRAMWAYS CO LTD

Horse-drawn bus services began in Paris in 1828 with an omnibus. New York City had its first omnibus in 1825. London omnibuses, introduced in 1829, carried 22 passengers all inside, but later variants, like

this 1881 example, had seats on the roof. Its spiral staircase enabled ladies to climb aboard without revealing their ankles – earlier versions had a ladder, and traveling on top had involved an "indecent" climb.

By laying rails transportation operators reduced friction, so a single horse could do the work of two. Streetcars, or horse trams, first ran along the Bowery in New York in 1832. They were in use until the

end of the century, when other sources of power began to replace the tired animals. Electric streetcars arrived just in time: removing the plentiful horse droppings each night was a huge and smelly problem.

Two-Wheeled Transportation

1817 Draisine

The first machine recognizable as a bicycle was the *Draisine*, or "running machine," made of wood and metal by German engineer Karl von Drais.

1818 Hobby horse

Steering mechanism

Leather saddle

Dennis Johnson of England made a similar kind of machine, called the "hobby horse," but it was uncomfortable and hard to ride.

1839 Macmillan's bicycle

Wooden frame

Push pedals

Scottish blacksmith Kirkpatrick Macmillan had the idea of adding pedals to the hobby horse. It went so fast that he was fined for "furious driving."

1865 Lallement's bicycle

Rotary pedals

Smaller rear wheel

Frenchman Pierre Lallement improved on Macmillan's machine by adding rotary pedals, which turned the larger front wheel of the bike.

1886 Starley's Safety

Diamond-shaped frame

Equal-sized wheels

Starley's Safety bicycle combined for the first time equal-sized wheels, a diamond-shaped frame, and direct steering to the front wheel.

1880s Tricycles

Two large front wheels

Tricycles were popular in the 1880s, but were dangerous because the rider could not leap clear in an accident. Many riders were badly injured as a result.

1880s Ladies' model tricycle

Steering handle

This unusual type of ladies' tricycle was steered with a spade-shaped handle that turned the small wheels at the front and back of the vehicle.

1894 Hildebrand and Wolfmüller

Hand brake

Early motorcycles were individually made: the Hildebrand and Wolfmüller was the first to go into regular production, in Germany.

1912 Indian

Two cylinder V-mounted engine

Motorcycles made by the Indian Company of the United States, such as this V-twin, were models of ruggedness, power, and reliability.

1914-18 Douglas

Carrier

Headlight

During World War I, Douglas motorcycles provided the British army with speedy mounts for messengers and troops, particularly at the front lines.

1920s Roadster

Chain guard

Hand brake

By the 1920s, bicycles had evolved into a cheap form of mass transportation. This style of roadster was used worldwide, but particularly in India and the Far East.

1927 Norton CSI

Leather helmet and goggles

British machines, such as this Norton CSI, dominated motorcycle sports right through the 1920s, winning both road and track races at home and abroad.

1950s Harley-Davidson

Large engine

Leather carrier

Harley-Davidsons have been the best-known American motorcycles since the 1950s. They are fast and powerful, and are used by many police forces.

1960s Moulton small-wheel

Small wheels

By rethinking the bicycle's design, Alex Moulton devised a more stable, small-wheeled machine that became hugely popular in the 1960s.

1960s Honda

Lightweight frame

Inexpensive Honda commuter bikes helped establish the reputation of Japanese manufacturers and make motorcycles family machines.

1970s Tandem

Dual chain drive

Multi-seater bicycles are now rare. Early ones carried as many as five people, but today the two-seater tandem boasts the maximum passenger load.

1868 Michaux steam bicycle

Belt drive

Steam engine

Lallement's employers, the Michaux brothers, added a steam engine. The alcohol-burning engine was placed just below the seat.

1870 Penny Farthing

Small rear wheel for balance

Without gears, wheel size limited a bike's speed, so Englishman James Starley's Penny Farthing had a giant drive wheel.

1879 Lawson's Bicyclette

Chain drive

Another Englishman, Harry Lawson, introduced the world's first chain drive. His Bicyclette even had a primitive hand brake.

1885 Daimler's motorbike

Wooden wheel

Gasoline engine

Germans Daimler and Maybach built a gas-driven motorbike. It had wooden wheels like a cart and included training wheels for balance.

1894 Bernardi

Powered trailer

Normal bicycle

Italian Enrico Bernardi's engine was too heavy to fit on a bike, so he built a powered trailer that pushed the entire contraption from behind.

1901 Werner

Front-mounted engine

Belt drive

A French Werner machine mounted the engine over the front wheel. Small French motorbikes still use this unusual arrangement.

1901 Werner brothers

Central engine

The French Werner brothers, Michael and Eugene, pioneered the modern low central engine and hand throttle in their 1901 model motorbike.

1910 FN

Multi-cylinder engine

The FN motorcycle from Belgium was among the first to have a multi-cylinder engine fitted into the frame as most modern bikes do.

1930 Brough Superior

Distinctive fantail exhaust pipes

Powerful engine

This Brough Superior from England was fast, well-made, and elegant – but its high price meant that only the rich could afford to ride one.

1930s Gilera

Wheel cover

In the 1930s, this Italian Gilera challenged British bikes for speed.

1939-45 BMW and sidecar

Spare tire

Gun

World War II motorcycles moved troops, weapons, and casualties. This German BMW and sidecar is fitted with a medium-caliber machine gun.

1940s-50s Vespa

Covered engine

Flat footrest

Covering the engine made motorbikes less noisy, and the Italian Vespas of the late 1940s and 50s were stylish fashion accessories for young people.

1980s-90s Racing bike

Bent-over riding position

Very light frame

Road racing bikes use aluminum alloys to reduce weight and lessen strain on the cyclist. Narrow high-pressure tires also make pedaling easier.

1980s Dirt bike

Protective fenders

Motorcycles have evolved into touring, racing, and off-road types. Dirt bikes have protection against flying stones. They also have rugged tires.

1980s Mountain bike

Strong frame

Deep-tread tires

Mountain bikes became popular in the 1980s. They have tires with deep treads, lightweight frames, and special gears to make hill climbing easier.

1992 Lotus

Streamlined helmet

Streamlined wheel design

This Lotus bike is the latest in racing design. It has an ultralight frame and streamlined wheels to cut wind resistance as much as possible and increase speed.

CARS

15th century Leonardo da Vinci

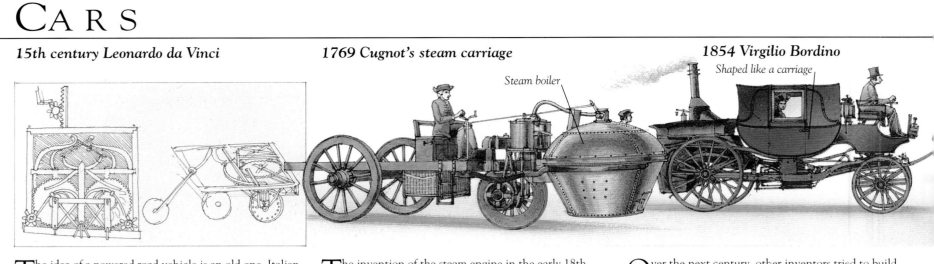

The idea of a powered road vehicle is an old one. Italian artist and engineer Leonardo da Vinci (1452-1519) sketched carts with mechanical drives in his notebooks. The diagrams suggest that the muscle power of the passengers drove the carts along the road.

1769 Cugnot's steam carriage

Steam boiler

The invention of the steam engine in the early 18th century made possible cars that were truly self-propelled. French artillery officer Nicolas Joseph Cugnot (1725-1804) was probably the first to build a steam-powered car, in 1769. It moved along at walking pace.

1854 Virgilio Bordino

Shaped like a carriage

Over the next century, other inventors tried to build steam carriages, but few had any more success than Cugnot. This passenger carriage, built in 1854 by Italian Virgilio Bordino, was just as slow, and it burned 66 lbs (30 kg) of coal each hour.

1901 Oldsmobile Curved dash Runabout
1911 Model 71 Stanley Steamer
1907-1925 Rolls-Royce Silver Ghost

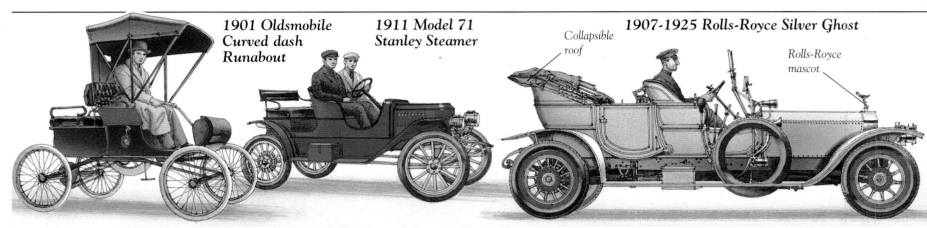

Collapsible roof

Rolls-Royce mascot

Ransom Olds established one of the first American automobile companies in 1897. In 1901, the Oldsmobile company started to make the Curved dash Runabout, using a production-line technique that all other car manufacturers copied.

American twins F.E. and F.O. Stanley built a series of steam cars that were capable of speeds up to 75 mph (120 km/h). The decline in horse transportation hindered them: fewer horses meant fewer drinking troughs and steamer drivers needed them to refill their water tanks.

British manufacturer Rolls-Royce began building cars in 1906. The launch in 1907 of the Silver Ghost established the company's reputation as a builder of the most luxurious cars in the world. Of 7,000 Ghosts made between 1907 and 1925, about 1,000 are still running.

1934 Citroën Traction Avant
1935-6 Auburn 851 Speedster
1937 Volkswagen

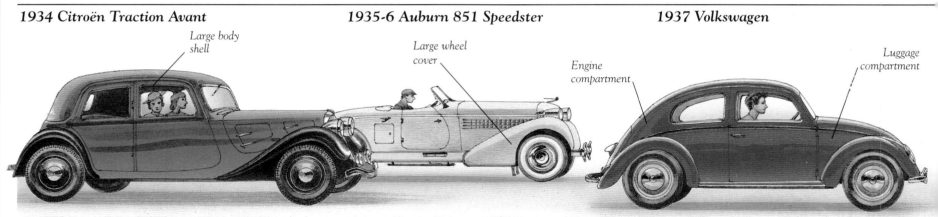

Large body shell

Large wheel cover

Engine compartment

Luggage compartment

Until the 1930s, manufacturers built cars much like carriages. This pattern changed forever when the French Citroën Company introduced its Traction Avant in 1934. It had a monocoque (one-piece) body shell, and was the first car to have front-wheel drive.

Shiny exhaust pipes bursting from the hood of the American Auburn 851 Speedster make it instantly identifiable. The car quickly became a classic, and though it remains a favorite among replica builders, the original model never made a profit.

Austrian-born German dictator Adolf Hitler (1889-1945) ordered in 1934 the creation of the Volkswagen ("people's car") so that motor travel would no longer be a luxury. Production of the car began in 1945 after Hitler's death. Since then, more than 21 million have been sold.

1955 Citroën DS 19
1959 Morris Mini Minor
1962 Ferrari

Streamlined shape

Small wheel

Aerodynamic shape slices through wind resistance

The shape of the Citroën DS 19 looks modern, but the car was a radical departure with tradition on its 1955 debut. The DS 19 used hydraulic power extensively, and had a suspension system that was adjustable to suit different loads and road conditions.

By completely rethinking the automobile, Turkish-born Briton Alec Issigonis created the very popular Mini Minor. Though very economical and ideally suited to narrow, crowded British roads, the Mini was cramped, noisy, and uncomfortable for long journeys.

Sheer speed has always appealed to car drivers in search of excitement. As a Grand-Prix racing driver, Italian Enzo Ferrari could understand this appeal. From 1940 onward, he designed some of the world's fastest (and most expensive) road cars.

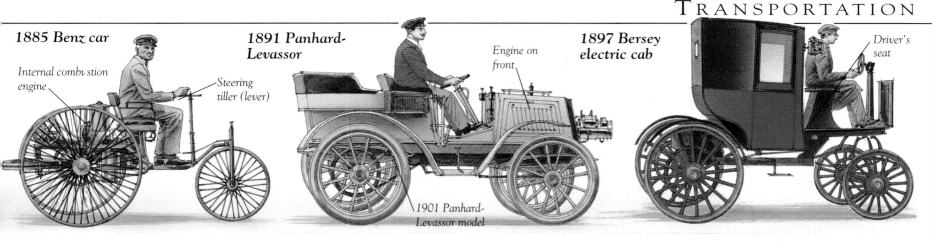

1885 Benz car

Internal combustion engine

Steering tiller (lever)

1891 Panhard-Levassor

Engine on front

1901 Panhard-Levassor model

1897 Bersey electric cab

Driver's seat

Success came when engineers discarded the steam engine, and instead used a gasoline-fueled internal combustion engine. German Karl Friedrich Benz (1844-1929) was the first to build a really practical car. His three-wheeler traveled at running speed.

René Panhard and Emile Levassor began to build vehicles in 1891. Their 1895 model provided the pattern for the modern car. It had a wheel at each corner, the engine at the front, a pedal clutch, a gearbox, and rear-wheel drive.

Electricity briefly competed with gas as a fuel source. In London, the Electric Cab Company ran a fleet of battery-powered taxis with a range of 50 miles (80 km). The driver braked by reversing the battery connections, so the cells recharged as the cab slowed down!

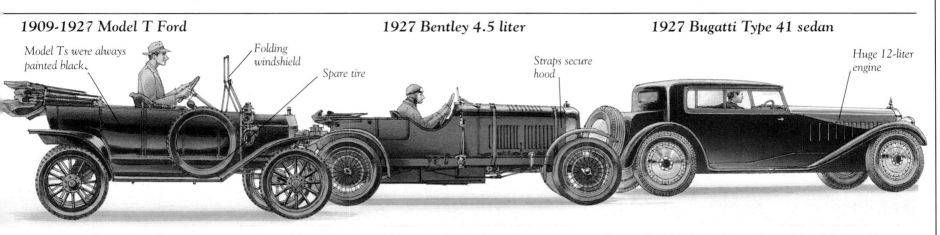

1909-1927 Model T Ford

Model Ts were always painted black.

Folding windshield

Spare tire

1927 Bentley 4.5 liter

Straps secure hood

1927 Bugatti Type 41 sedan

Huge 12-liter engine

In contrast to the costly Rolls-Royce, Henry Ford's Model T was cheap: he called it a "car for the great multitude." Introduced in 1909, the "Tin Lizzie" cost $850. By 1925 the price had dropped to $290 – about 9 weeks' wages for a skilled manual worker.

Success on the racetrack is the best advertisement a car can have. Britain's Bentley Company built successful sports cars that won five Le Mans 24-hour races. This 4.5-liter "blower" model is still everyone's idea of a perfect vintage car.

The 22-ft (6.7-m) long Bugatti "Royale" Type 41 was the biggest car ever. Its 12-liter engine was powerful enough to drive a train. Only six were built, and they were the most expensive vehicles in the world. Even second-hand Royales still set world record prices at auctions.

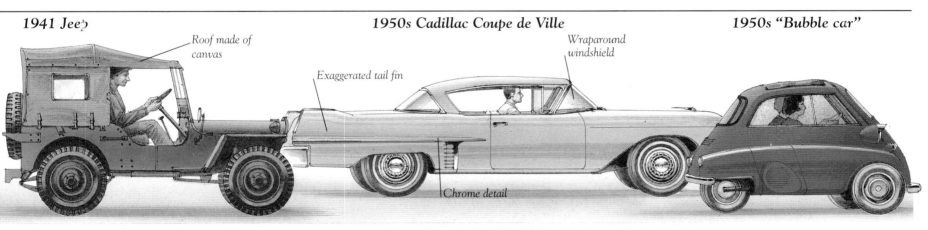

1941 Jeep

Roof made of canvas

1950s Cadillac Coupe de Ville

Wraparound windshield

Exaggerated tail fin

Chrome detail

1950s "Bubble car"

The Willys Jeep took its name from GP – short for general purpose – and from Eugene the Jeep, a cartoon character. In World War II (1939-45), 500,000 Jeeps transported US soldiers, but the uncomfortable ride gave many "jeep-disease," a painful spine injury.

American designer Harley Earl (1893-1969) introduced the sweeping tail fins, chrome, and two-tone paint finishes for which the cars of the 1950s are famous. His 1957 Coupe de Ville design for Cadillac was among the last of the giant gas-guzzlers.

Postwar fuel rationing and traffic congestion meant that 1950s car design in Europe could not have been more different. The Italian-German Issetta cars, nicknamed "bubble cars," took compactness to an extreme: a tiny 236-cubic centimeter engine drove this two-seater.

1987-88 Porsche 959

Airfoil

1993 Nissan Micra

Compact shape

1990s Formula I

Airfoil

Open cockpit

Most car manufacturers change their models each year, but a few designs remain constant. The profile of the Porsche 911 has barely changed since its 1963 introduction, and it is recognizable even in special-edition cars such as the 200-mph (320-km/h) 959 model.

Modern production cars show none of the style and individuality of their ancestors: computer design and the quest for low air resistance ensures that they all look similar. However, cars such as the Nissan Micra are more reliable and economical than ever before.

Designed to compete in motor races at speeds of up to 200 mph (320 km/h), Formula I cars are built by specialized teams of designers and engineers. Air rushing over the wing-shaped airfoil on the front of the car pushes down and holds the car firmly on the track.

STEAM LOCOMOTIVES

1804 Richard Trevithick's locomotive

1825 Locomotion

1829 Rocket

Chimney

Boiler

Cylinder

Steam railroad transportation began when Englishman Richard Trevithick built the first locomotive to run on rails. He made the engine's fire burn hotter by directing the exhaust steam up a chimney. This created enough steam in the boiler to make the engine run successfully.

The earliest locomotives hauled freight; passenger trains didn't exist for another 21 years. George Stephenson's Locomotion pulled the first passenger train on the Stockton to Darlington Railway in England. The trains traveled at the alarming speed of 8 mph (12 km/h)!

To choose a locomotive for another new English railroad, the Liverpool and Manchester, the owners held a race in 1829. A machine called the Rocket, built by George Stephenson's son, Robert, won the contest, reaching nearly 30 mph (50 km/h).

1850s French Crampton

Driving wheel

1860 American

Sandbox

Smokestack

English engineer T.R. Crampton's locomotives were most successful in France. The locos were so famous that among military cadets *"Prenez le Crampton"* (taking the Crampton) was slang for a night out. This type of engine set a speed record of 89.5 mph (144 km/h) in 1889.

The American class of locomotives evolved to suit the special conditions of United States railroads; long unfenced tracks. These engines had a distinctive cowcatcher on the front to push wandering livestock out of the way. After an 1836 plague of grasshoppers caused tracks

(in Pennsylvania) to become slippery with squashed insects, all trains began carrying sand to grit the rails. Most of these locomotives burned wood, and the huge smokestack was designed to catch hot embers and prevent trackside grass fires.

Fireman's platform

1900 Camelback

Cab

1906 Royal Prussian Union Railways P8

The curiously shaped American Camelback locomotive had a cab mounted across the boiler, halfway along the locomotive. The locomotive's engineers chose this odd design to increase the size of the firebox so that

the fireman could burn lower quality coal. The position of the cab gave the driver better visibility, but left the fireman exposed on a small platform at the rear. At this time, American locomotives still had cowcatchers.

This locomotive was part of a class of powerful, well-built engines that hauled both passenger and goods trains in Germany for many years. They were renowned for their reliability and lack of repairs.

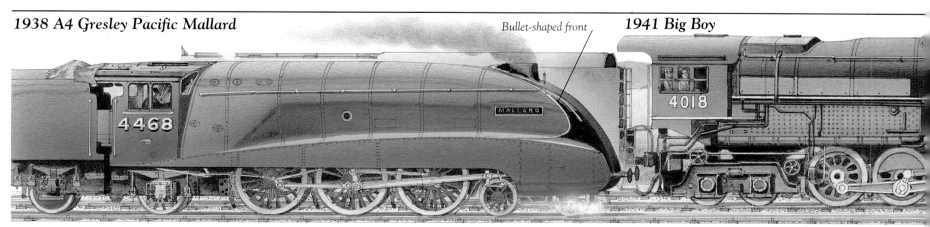

1938 A4 Gresley Pacific Mallard

Bullet-shaped front

1941 Big Boy

The world's fastest steam locomotive was a British engine, Mallard. Also designed by Gresley, Mallard briefly reached a top speed of 126 mph (202 km/h) on July 3, 1938. To reduce air resistance and boost speed, Mallard was streamlined: the front of the locomotive was

smooth and rounded, like a bullet. For the famous speed trial, Mallard hauled a train with a dynamometer car attached. This was a car filled with instruments to measure the locomotive's performance. During the trial, parts of the locomotive overheated and were damaged.

As freight trains grew in length, they needed larger locomotives to pull them. US railroads needed especially big locomotives because they covered vast areas, often with steep inclines. So in 1940, the Union Pacific Railroads ordered 25 huge Big Boy locomotives. These

1831 DeWitt Clinton

1835 Planet

1851 Lord of the Isles

Water tank

Driver

The popularity of railroads rapidly spread to the United States. One of the earliest American locomotives, DeWitt Clinton, was the first to carry a water tank in the base of its tender (coal truck). The locomotive pulled cars on the Mohawk and Hudson Railroads.

To convert the to-and-fro movement of the piston to a rotary motion to turn the wheels, the Planet class of locomotives from the 1830s used a system of twin gears. The smaller gear turned around the larger – just as a planet, such as the Earth, orbits the Sun.

Britain's Great Western Railway company made their Lord of the Isles locomotive famous when they displayed it at the Great Exhibition. This was a huge mid-century show of industrial products, held in a specially built "Crystal Palace" in Hyde Park, London.

1870 Stirling Single

1884 Vittorio Emanuelle II

1893 No. 999

Driving wheel

British railroads used heavier rails than American. This meant that British locomotives could use fewer, larger driving wheels. The distinctive Stirling locomotive had a single pair of driving wheels nearly 8 ft (2.5 m) in diameter. It could reach speeds of 60 mph (100 km/h).

The railroads of northern Italy wind around mountain-sides, so Italian locomotives were specially designed for steep slopes and tight curves. The Vittorio Emanuelle II, named after the first king of Italy, was the model for many later Italian engines.

The American No. 999 took part in a speed trial over one mile (1.6 km) of track in New York State. It was clocked at 100 mph (160 km/h), the first locomotive to reach such a speed. Even in regular service, it went from New York City to Buffalo in 8½ hours.

1922 A3 Gresley Pacific Flying Scotsman

1920s Super Pacific

The powerful Pacific class locomotives were first developed in 1886. They were soon in service all over the world. This famous British locomotive, the Flying Scotsman, hauled passengers on the longest nonstop rail

journey in the world, from London to Edinburgh. The A3 class was designed by the engineer Sir Nigel Gresley for the Great Northern Railway, which became part of the London and North Eastern Railway in 1923.

This French design included many technical advances, such as "compounding" (using both high and low pressure steam to drive the locomotive). These engines hauled many French trains, including the Orient Express.

1960 Evening Star

gigantic engines were nearly 131 ft (40 m) long. Because of their size, these engines had trouble traveling around bends. So that they could cope with curved track, the locomotives were articulated – the two sets of eight driving wheels moved independently.

By the 1960s, powerful diesel locomotives were starting to replace steam locomotives in Europe and the Americas. Evening Star was the last steam engine to be built in Britain, and when it was completed in March 1960, there were more than 14,000 steam locomotives at work on

British tracks. Evening Star was taken out of service in 1965, and just three years later, diesel and electric locomotives had completely replaced steam. However, many steam locomotives are preserved and lovingly cared for by enthusiasts today.

Boats and sailing ships

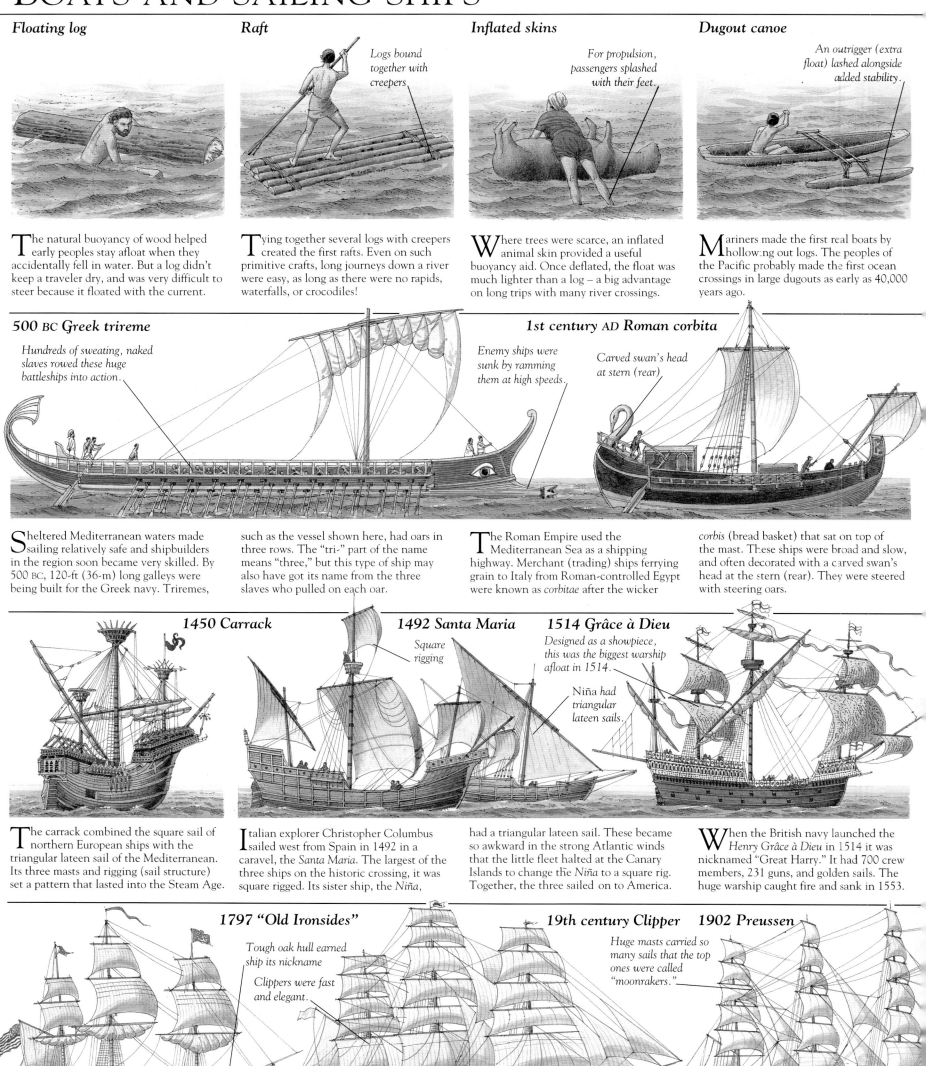

Floating log

Tying together several logs with creepers created the first rafts.

The natural buoyancy of wood helped early peoples stay afloat when they accidentally fell in water. But a log didn't keep a traveler dry, and was very difficult to steer because it floated with the current.

Raft

Logs bound together with creepers

Tying together several logs with creepers created the first rafts. Even on such primitive crafts, long journeys down a river were easy, as long as there were no rapids, waterfalls, or crocodiles!

Inflated skins

For propulsion, passengers splashed with their feet.

Where trees were scarce, an inflated animal skin provided a useful buoyancy aid. Once deflated, the float was much lighter than a log – a big advantage on long trips with many river crossings.

Dugout canoe

An outrigger (extra float) lashed alongside added stability.

Mariners made the first real boats by hollowing out logs. The peoples of the Pacific probably made the first ocean crossings in large dugouts as early as 40,000 years ago.

500 BC Greek trireme

Hundreds of sweating, naked slaves rowed these huge battleships into action.

Enemy ships were sunk by ramming them at high speeds.

Sheltered Mediterranean waters made sailing relatively safe and shipbuilders in the region soon became very skilled. By 500 BC, 120-ft (36-m) long galleys were being built for the Greek navy. Triremes, such as the vessel shown here, had oars in three rows. The "tri-" part of the name means "three," but this type of ship may also have got its name from the three slaves who pulled on each oar.

1st century AD Roman corbita

Carved swan's head at stern (rear)

The Roman Empire used the Mediterranean Sea as a shipping highway. Merchant (trading) ships ferrying grain to Italy from Roman-controlled Egypt were known as *corbitae* after the wicker *corbis* (bread basket) that sat on top of the mast. These ships were broad and slow, and often decorated with a carved swan's head at the stern (rear). They were steered with steering oars.

1450 Carrack

The carrack combined the square sail of northern European ships with the triangular lateen sail of the Mediterranean. Its three masts and rigging (sail structure) set a pattern that lasted into the Steam Age.

1492 Santa Maria

Square rigging

Italian explorer Christopher Columbus sailed west from Spain in 1492 in a caravel, the *Santa Maria*. The largest of the three ships on the historic crossing, it was square rigged. Its sister ship, the *Niña*, had a triangular lateen sail. These became so awkward in the strong Atlantic winds that the little fleet halted at the Canary Islands to change the *Niña* to a square rig. Together, the three sailed on to America.

1514 Grâce à Dieu

Designed as a showpiece, this was the biggest warship afloat in 1514.

Niña had triangular lateen sails.

When the British navy launched the *Henry Grâce à Dieu* in 1514 it was nicknamed "Great Harry." It had 700 crew members, 231 guns, and golden sails. The huge warship caught fire and sank in 1553.

1797 "Old Ironsides"

Tough oak hull earned ship its nickname

Clippers were fast and elegant.

The *Constitution* was one of six frigates built to form the US Navy. It was saved from the scrap heap in 1830 by Oliver Wendell Holmes's poem "Old Ironsides," which appealed for its preservation.

19th century Clipper

Huge masts carried so many sails that the top ones were called "moonrakers."

Early steamships were slow, so on ocean routes where speed was vital, sailing ships were still competitive well into the Steam Age. Clipper ships were the fastest. To reduce friction, their long, narrow hulls kept the area in contact with the water to a minimum. Though fast and elegant, clippers were doomed because they required large crews to sail them and had little space for cargo.

1902 Preussen

Commercial sailing ships just survived into the 20th century. The last of them were huge, steel-hulled barques with an enormous sail area. They were usually three- or four-masted, but the biggest, the

Frame boat

A coating of pitch kept the joints watertight.

The frame boat is equally ancient. It was built like a basket covered in animal skins; a coating of pitch sealed the joints. Boats like this, called *cufas*, were in use on the Tigris River until very recently.

Reed boat

Spongy reed stems trap air, providing buoyancy.

Reeds grow near water and are an ideal material for boatbuilding. The reed boats that the people of Bolivia paddle today on Lake Titicaca have hardly changed since prehistoric times.

4000 BC Sailboats

A taut rope stretched along the flexible hull kept it rigid

Pacific island peoples may have been the first to use sails: their ocean voyages were too long for a rowboat. However, the first real evidence of sailing comes not from Oceania, but from Egypt. Boatbuilders on the Nile River added a mast and sails to reed boats. By 2500 BC they were building wooden boats that were seaworthy enough to sail out of the Nile River and into the Mediterranean beyond.

800 Arab dhow

Dhows were lateen-rigged (triangular-sailed) vessels.

Like the Mediterranean, the Persian Gulf and the Red Sea are safe for sailing, so people of the Arabian Peninsula became legendary sailors. They crossed the Indian Ocean in crafts Europeans called *dhows*.

1000 Viking longboat

Longboats had sails as well as sailors rowing.

The Norse people of Scandinavia sailed as far afield as North America in their distinctive longboats. Later vessels had sails. Boats were very important in Viking culture, and chiefs were buried in them.

1100 Chinese junk

Battens reinforced joints supporting the sails.

Many basic maritime inventions are Chinese. Junks had a rudder (rather than a steering oar), sails with battens, and watertight compartments many centuries before they were used on Western ships.

1400 Venetian galleasse

The width of the galleasse made it difficult to row.

Designed for sails and oars, the galleasse suffered from the defects of both forms of power. Its width made the ship harder to row than a galley, and the hull was weaker than that of a pure sailing vessel.

1587 Ark Royal

In the 16th century, Britain's strong navy dominated the world's oceans. When the Spanish Armada (invasion force) neared Britain in 1588, the *Ark Royal* led the destruction of the Spanish threat.

1650 Dutch East Indiaman

To dominate trade with the Far East, Europeans built huge armed ships called East Indiamen. The ships of Britain and Holland were the grandest and merchants grew rich from their voyages.

1728 Bucentaur

The doge (ruler) of Venice threw a ring into the water from Bucentaur during the ceremony.

The official galley of the doge (ruler) of Venice was *Bucentaur*. Its most important yearly voyage was the Wedding of the Sea, 40 days after Easter. The ceremony honored Venice's long link with the sea.

1765 HMS Victory

In the 18th century, the *Victory* ensured that Britain ruled the waves. Horatio Nelson commanded the British fleet from its decks, defeating French and Spanish fleets at the Battle of Trafalgar in 1805.

German ship *Preussen*, had five masts. It sailed at amazing speeds when the wind was in the right direction. The ship's power so terrified the crew that few would make more than one voyage in the *Preussen*.

1920s Bluenose

Schooners had fore-and-aft rigged sails.

The fore-and-aft rig (sail arrangement) and slim hull of the *Bluenose* helped it become a successful ocean racer. It was originally built as a fishing schooner, working on Canada's Grand Banks.

Ocean racer

Ocean racers like this one can cut through the waves at 25 knots.

Almost all modern sailing vessels are now used for pleasure or sport. Most have a single hull, like this example, but some are twin-hulled catamarans, which are based on an ancient Pacific design.

1980 Shin Aitoku Maru

Sails on the Japanese ship Shin Aitoku Maru help push the ship forward in the water.

A sudden rise in oil prices in the 1970s made ship designers look again at sail power as a way of saving fuel. In favorable conditions, computer-controlled sails can cut fuel consumption in half.

SHIPS UNDER POWER

Oxen-powered ship

Oxen walking in circles around a capstan

1736 Jonathan Hulls's tug

The inventors of steam engines at the beginning of the 18th century predicted that the new power source would be useful for driving ships.

1807 Clermont

1816 Charles-Philippe

Clermont

Charles-Philippe

An unknown author drew the very first powered ship in the fourth century AD. Oxen in the hold turned a capstan, which powered the paddle wheels.

Englishman Jonathan Hulls was first to patent a steam-powered tugboat in 1736 for towing warships out of harbors. However, Hulls's boat was never built.

The first practical steam-powered boat was invented by the American engineer Robert Fulton. The engine drove paddle wheels to propel the boat forward.

Built by the French inventor Claude D.-E. d'Abban Jouffroy, the steamboat *Charles-Philippe* carried passengers in a regular service on the Seine River in 1816.

1858 Great Eastern

This ship was nicknamed "The Floating City."

1861 Warrior

The Warrior was the world's first all-iron battleship.

1862 Merrimack and Monitor

Confederate ship Merrimack

Union ship Monitor

Like the *Great Western* and *Great Britain*, the *Great Eastern* was built to the designs of English engineer Isambard Kingdom Brunel. It was the largest vessel to be built in the 19th century and became a cable-laying ship.

The British navy was slow to build "ironclad" warships, preferring wooden ones. But news that the French navy was to build iron ships forced the British into action. The *Warrior* was completed ahead of its French rivals.

The first battle between steam-propelled ironclads took place in the American Civil War (1861-1865). The Confederate *Merrimack* and the Union *Monitor* clashed off the coast of Virginia. The battle was inconclusive.

1906 Dreadnought

Britain's Dreadnought, launched in 1906, was built in a year and a day and set the pattern for all battleships that followed.

1906 Mauretania

The speed advantage of turbine power was essential on the North Atlantic route, where competition for passengers was fierce.

Mauretania was launched in 1906.

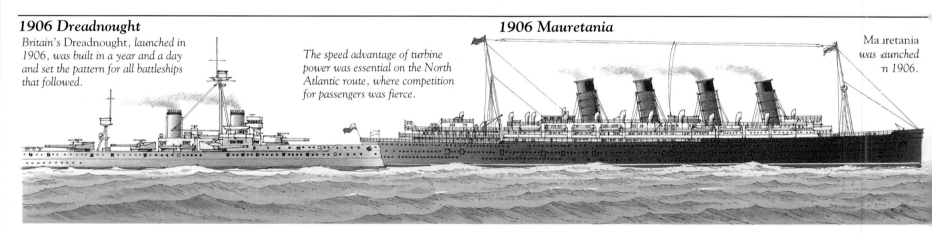

The first large battleship to be powered by a turbine was the *Dreadnought*. It was revolutionary in other ways, too: it was very fast, and was the first warship equipped only with big guns. Other ships of the time had a mixture of different guns, but all of *Dreadnought*'s ten guns fired the same 12-inch (300-mm) caliber shells.

Competition among passenger shipping lines was as fierce in 1906 as it is among airlines today. Two ships on Britain's Cunard line were among the first to abandon piston engines. The successful *Mauretania* soon took the Blue Riband (a fantasy trophy for the fastest Atlantic crossing) and held it until 1929.

Icebreaker

This icebreaker is Canada's Louis St. Laurent, launched in 1969.

Hovercraft

Neither ships nor airplanes, hovercraft float just above the waves on cushions of air.

Hydrofoil

The wings of the hydrofoil are hidden underwater when it is traveling slowly.

Supertanker

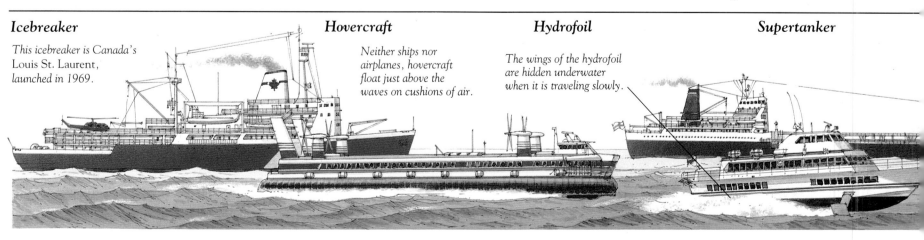

To keep shipping lanes open in polar regions, icebreakers lead the way. These special ships have extra strong hulls to resist the crushing pressure of ice.

Hovercraft are the fastest of marine craft, capable of over 75 knots (87 mph). Most are used as ferries on short routes, such as across the English Channel.

A hydrofoil rides on wings that lift it as it picks up speed. The craft are unstable in heavy seas, but make speedy ferries or "river taxis" on inland waterways.

The world's biggest ships are oil tankers, and the biggest oil tankers are the ultra-large crude carriers. These vast vessels are nearly 1,500 ft (half a

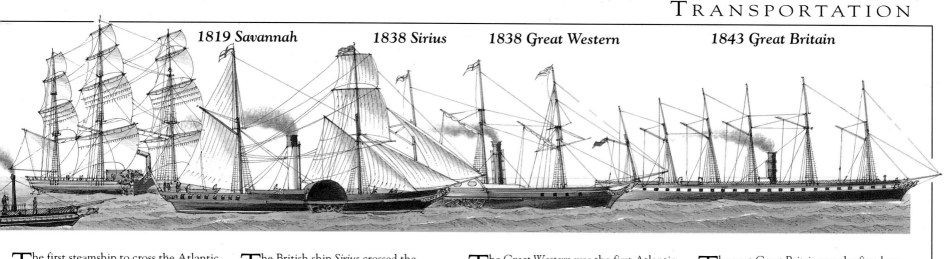

1819 Savannah **1838 Sirius** **1838 Great Western** **1843 Great Britain**

The first steamship to cross the Atlantic was the *Savannah*. However, it sailed most of the way, using steam power for only 85 hours of the month-long trip.

The British ship *Sirius* crossed the Atlantic without using its sails. It ran out of fuel before arriving. The crew burned furniture to keep the steam pressure up.

The *Great Western* was the first Atlantic steamer in regular service. Built of oak, it was also the first ship able to carry enough coal for the entire crossing.

The vast *Great Britain* was the first large iron ship, and the first to be powered by screw propellers rather than paddles. It still had six masts, though.

1871 Devastation **1896 Turbinia** **1901 King Edward**

Devastation's 8-in (20-cm) steel armor was even thicker at crucial points.

Parsons demonstrated his ship by tearing between the lines of slow-moving battleships at Queen Victoria's 1897 Jubilee naval review.

Turbine power made possible faster ships, so it was adopted for merchant shipping as well as navy vessels.

Less than a decade after this inconclusive clash, warships had begun to take on their modern form. The first ocean-going battleship without masts was Britain's *Devastation*. It had steel armor backed by teak timber.

All early steamships used piston engines, but British engineer Charles Parsons invented a rotary marine turbine engine, which he fitted to the *Turbinia*. It powered the ship at the unheard of speed of 34.5 knots.

The first turbine-powered merchant ship was a passenger steamer, the *King Edward*. In speed trials, it made 20.5 knots, beating its near-identical (but piston-and-paddle-powered) sister ship by two knots.

1910 Vulcanus **1941 Aircraft carrier**

The first ship to be powered by a diesel engine was the Dutch oil tanker Vulcanus.

Today, carriers are less popular because their size makes them an easy target for missiles and smart bombs.

Oil began to replace coal as a fuel for ships in the early years of the 20th century. At first coal-burning boilers were converted for oil, but the invention of the

diesel engine provided shipbuilders with a new source of power that used half the fuel of a turbine engine. The first vessel to be powered by diesel was the *Vulcanus*.

When pilot Eugène Ely took off from the deck of the US warship *Birmingham*, he united air and sea warfare. The Japanese launched the first custom-

built aircraft carrier, the *Hosho*, in 1922. British and American navies added runways to existing ships, and built carriers such as this US Essex class ship in 1941.

Ro-ro ferry **Tugboat** **Container ships**

Supertankers are so big that crew members bring bicycles on board to cycle between tasks.

Ro-ro ferries earned their name from the fact that vehicles roll onto them and then roll off.

Powerful tugs are vital in salvage work, recovering wrecked or stranded ships.

Containers are lifted from the deck straight into dockside storage or directly onto waiting trucks.

kilometer) long. Each tanker can carry up to half a million tons (tonnes) of crude oil, and tankers make up about half of the world's cargo-carrying capacity.

Motorists drive straight onto a modern ro-ro ferry, and off via a ramp at the other end. This is not a new idea; ro-ro ships carried trains in the 19th century.

The first practical steamship was designed for towing, and the tugboat is its modern descendant. Tugs move huge vessels in harbors and haul barges.

To speed the loading and unloading of freight at docks, container ships carry their cargo in standard-sized boxes. Special cranes lift the containers from the deck.

Airplanes

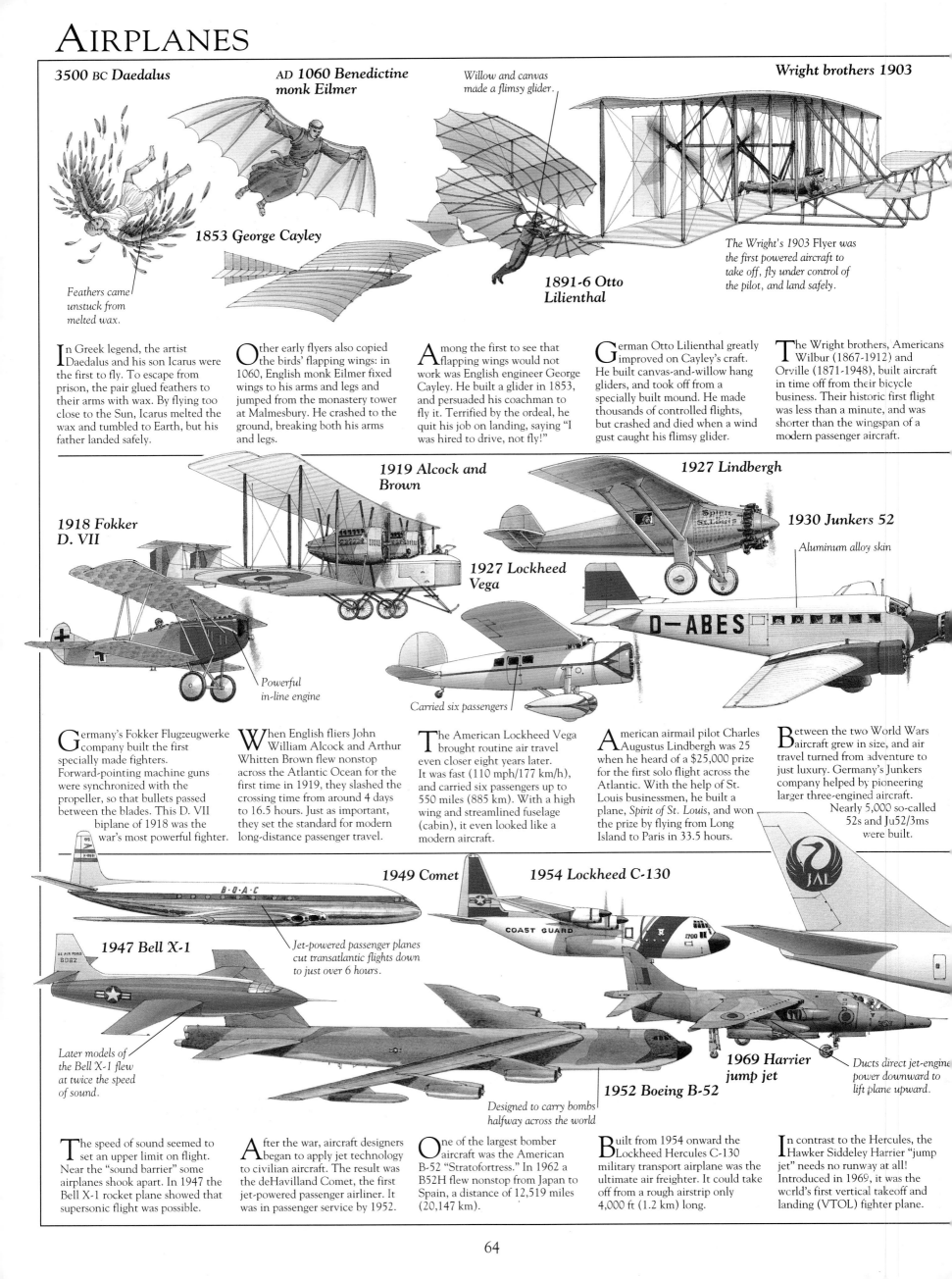

3500 BC Daedalus

Feathers came unstuck from melted wax.

AD 1060 Benedictine monk Eilmer

1853 George Cayley

Willow and canvas made a flimsy glider.

1891-6 Otto Lilienthal

Wright brothers 1903

The Wright's 1903 Flyer was the first powered aircraft to take off, fly under control of the pilot, and land safely.

In Greek legend, the artist Daedalus and his son Icarus were the first to fly. To escape from prison, the pair glued feathers to their arms with wax. By flying too close to the Sun, Icarus melted the wax and tumbled to Earth, but his father landed safely.

Other early flyers also copied the birds' flapping wings: in 1060, English monk Eilmer fixed wings to his arms and legs and jumped from the monastery tower at Malmesbury. He crashed to the ground, breaking both his arms and legs.

Among the first to see that flapping wings would not work was English engineer George Cayley. He built a glider in 1853, and persuaded his coachman to fly it. Terrified by the ordeal, he quit his job on landing, saying "I was hired to drive, not fly!"

German Otto Lilienthal greatly improved on Cayley's craft. He built canvas-and-willow hang gliders, and took off from a specially built mound. He made thousands of controlled flights, but crashed and died when a wind gust caught his flimsy glider.

The Wright brothers, Americans Wilbur (1867-1912) and Orville (1871-1948), built aircraft in time off from their bicycle business. Their historic first flight was less than a minute, and was shorter than the wingspan of a modern passenger aircraft.

1918 Fokker D. VII

1919 Alcock and Brown

1927 Lockheed Vega

1927 Lindbergh

1930 Junkers 52

Aluminum alloy skin

D-ABES

Powerful in-line engine

Carried six passengers

Germany's Fokker Flugzeugwerke company built the first specially made fighters. Forward-pointing machine guns were synchronized with the propeller, so that bullets passed between the blades. This D. VII biplane of 1918 was the war's most powerful fighter.

When English fliers John William Alcock and Arthur Whitten Brown flew nonstop across the Atlantic Ocean for the first time in 1919, they slashed the crossing time from around 4 days to 16.5 hours. Just as important, they set the standard for modern long-distance passenger travel.

The American Lockheed Vega brought routine air travel even closer eight years later. It was fast (110 mph/177 km/h), and carried six passengers up to 550 miles (885 km). With a high wing and streamlined fuselage (cabin), it even looked like a modern aircraft.

American airmail pilot Charles Augustus Lindbergh was 25 when he heard of a $25,000 prize for the first solo flight across the Atlantic. With the help of St. Louis businessmen, he built a plane, *Spirit of St. Louis*, and won the prize by flying from Long Island to Paris in 33.5 hours.

Between the two World Wars aircraft grew in size, and air travel turned from adventure to just luxury. Germany's Junkers company helped by pioneering larger three-engined aircraft. Nearly 5,000 so-called 52s and Ju52/3ms were built.

1947 Bell X-1

1949 Comet

Jet-powered passenger planes cut transatlantic flights down to just over 6 hours.

1954 Lockheed C-130

JAL

1969 Harrier jump jet

Ducts direct jet-engine power downward to lift plane upward.

1952 Boeing B-52

Designed to carry bombs halfway across the world

Later models of the Bell X-1 flew at twice the speed of sound.

The speed of sound seemed to set an upper limit on flight. Near the "sound barrier" some airplanes shook apart. In 1947 the Bell X-1 rocket plane showed that supersonic flight was possible.

After the war, aircraft designers began to apply jet technology to civilian aircraft. The result was the deHavilland Comet, the first jet-powered passenger airliner. It was in passenger service by 1952.

One of the largest bomber aircraft was the American B-52 "Stratofortress." In 1962 a B52H flew nonstop from Japan to Spain, a distance of 12,519 miles (20,147 km).

Built from 1954 onward the Lockheed Hercules C-130 military transport airplane was the ultimate air freighter. It could take off from a rough airstrip only 4,000 ft (1.2 km) long.

In contrast to the Hercules, the Hawker Siddeley Harrier "jump jet" needs no runway at all! Introduced in 1969, it was the world's first vertical takeoff and landing (VTOL) fighter plane.

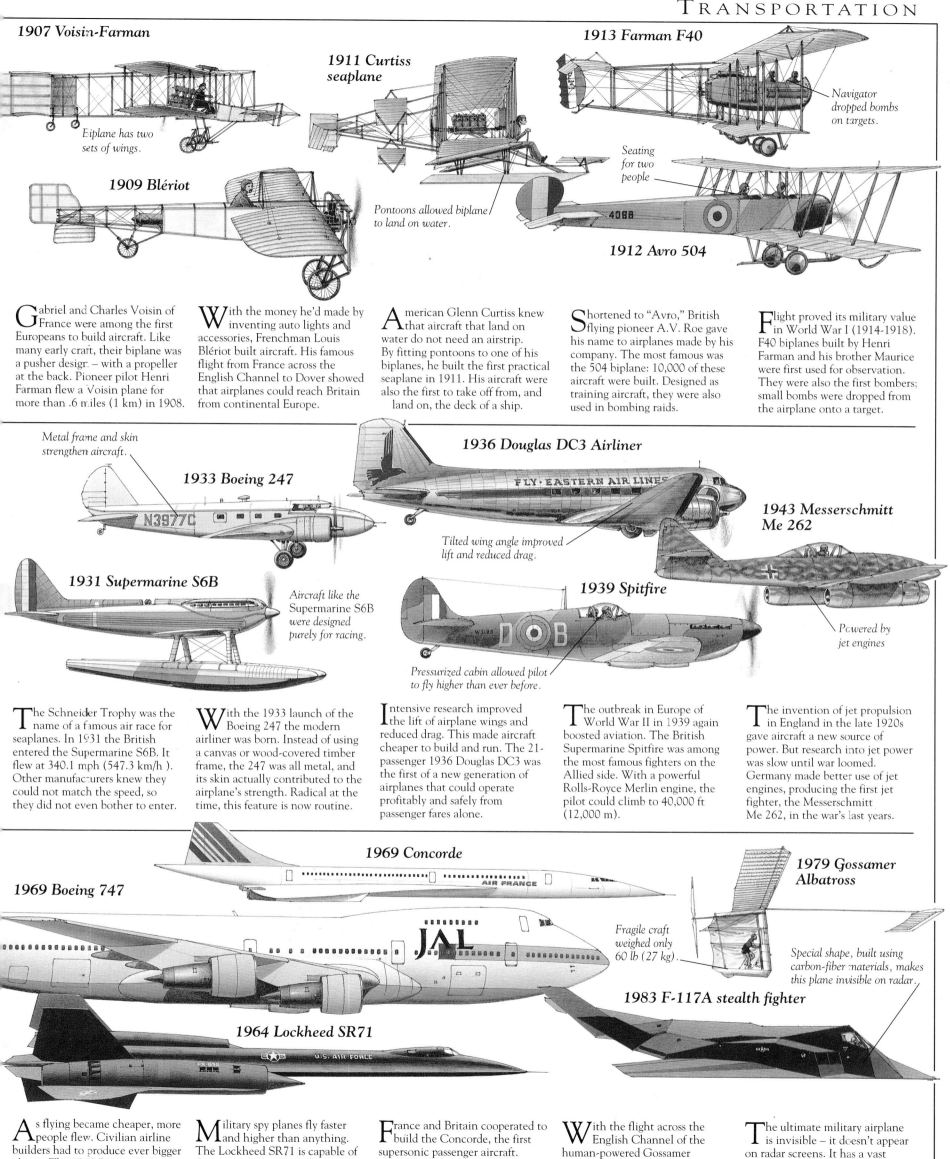

1907 Voisin-Farman

Biplane has two sets of wings.

1911 Curtiss seaplane

1913 Farman F40

Navigator dropped bombs on targets.

1909 Blériot

Pontoons allowed biplane to land on water.

Seating for two people

4068

1912 Avro 504

Gabriel and Charles Voisin of France were among the first Europeans to build aircraft. Like many early craft, their biplane was a pusher design – with a propeller at the back. Pioneer pilot Henri Farman flew a Voisin plane for more than .6 miles (1 km) in 1908.

With the money he'd made by inventing auto lights and accessories, Frenchman Louis Blériot built aircraft. His famous flight from France across the English Channel to Dover showed that airplanes could reach Britain from continental Europe.

American Glenn Curtiss knew that aircraft that land on water do not need an airstrip. By fitting pontoons to one of his biplanes, he built the first practical seaplane in 1911. His aircraft were also the first to take off from, and land on, the deck of a ship.

Shortened to "Avro," British flying pioneer A.V. Roe gave his name to airplanes made by his company. The most famous was the 504 biplane: 10,000 of these aircraft were built. Designed as training aircraft, they were also used in bombing raids.

Flight proved its military value in World War I (1914-1918). F40 biplanes built by Henri Farman and his brother Maurice were first used for observation. They were also the first bombers; small bombs were dropped from the airplane onto a target.

Metal frame and skin strengthen aircraft.

1933 Boeing 247

N3977C

1936 Douglas DC3 Airliner

FLY·EASTERN AIR LINES

Tilted wing angle improved lift and reduced drag.

1943 Messerschmitt Me 262

1931 Supermarine S6B

Aircraft like the Supermarine S6B were designed purely for racing.

1939 Spitfire

D ◎ B

Pressurized cabin allowed pilot to fly higher than ever before.

Powered by jet engines

The Schneider Trophy was the name of a famous air race for seaplanes. In 1931 the British entered the Supermarine S6B. It flew at 340.1 mph (547.3 km/h). Other manufacturers knew they could not match the speed, so they did not even bother to enter.

With the 1933 launch of the Boeing 247 the modern airliner was born. Instead of using a canvas or wood-covered timber frame, the 247 was all metal, and its skin actually contributed to the airplane's strength. Radical at the time, this feature is now routine.

Intensive research improved the lift of airplane wings and reduced drag. This made aircraft cheaper to build and run. The 21-passenger 1936 Douglas DC3 was the first of a new generation of airplanes that could operate profitably and safely from passenger fares alone.

The outbreak in Europe of World War II in 1939 again boosted aviation. The British Supermarine Spitfire was among the most famous fighters on the Allied side. With a powerful Rolls-Royce Merlin engine, the pilot could climb to 40,000 ft (12,000 m).

The invention of jet propulsion in England in the late 1920s gave aircraft a new source of power. But research into jet power was slow until war loomed. Germany made better use of jet engines, producing the first jet fighter, the Messerschmitt Me 262, in the war's last years.

1969 Concorde

AIR FRANCE

1979 Gossamer Albatross

1969 Boeing 747

JAL

Fragile craft weighed only 60 lb (27 kg).

Special shape, built using carbon-fiber materials, makes this plane invisible on radar.

1983 F-117A stealth fighter

U.S. AIR FORCE

1964 Lockheed SR71

As flying became cheaper, more people flew. Civilian airline builders had to produce ever bigger planes. The 1969 Boeing 747 carries 400 passengers. Once, an extra 274 were squeezed in.

Military spy planes fly faster and higher than anything. The Lockheed SR71 is capable of flying at 2,193 mph (3,530 km/h). Ironically, military spying nowadays is done by satellite!

France and Britain cooperated to build the Concorde, the first supersonic passenger aircraft. Scheduled flights began in 1976. The Concorde cut the trans-atlantic time to under 3 hours.

With the flight across the English Channel of the human-powered Gossamer Albatross, the myth of Daedalus came true. During the crossing, it almost skimmed the waves.

The ultimate military airplane is invisible – it doesn't appear on radar screens. It has a vast range, and can fly almost all the way around the world without stopping to refuel.

BALLOONS

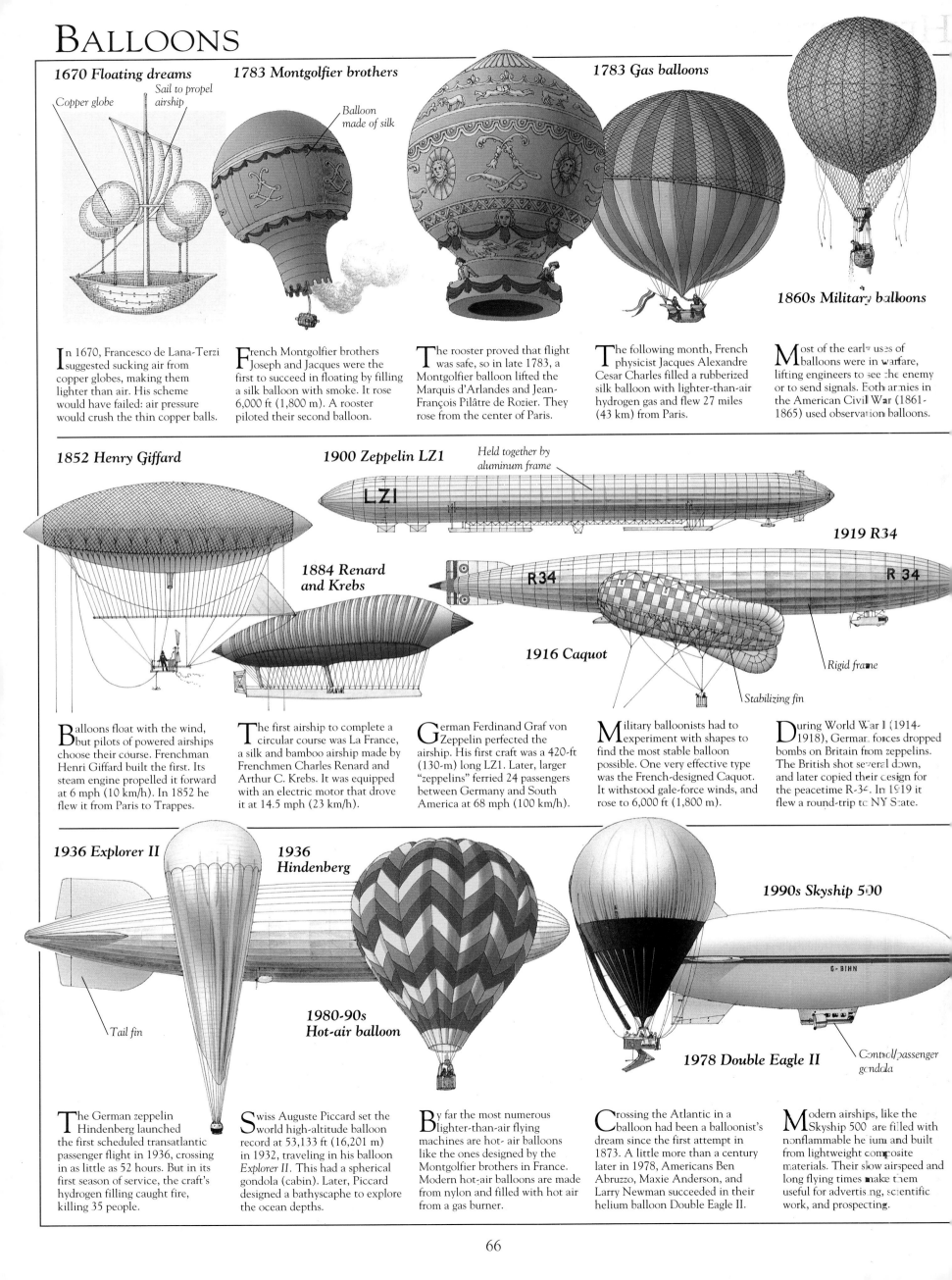

1670 Floating dreams

Copper globe

Sail to propel airship

In 1670, Francesco de Lana-Terzi suggested sucking air from copper globes, making them lighter than air. His scheme would have failed: air pressure would crush the thin copper balls.

1783 Montgolfier brothers

Balloon made of silk

French Montgolfier brothers Joseph and Jacques were the first to succeed in floating by filling a silk balloon with smoke. It rose 6,000 ft (1,800 m). A rooster piloted their second balloon.

1783 Gas balloons

The rooster proved that flight was safe, so in late 1783, a Montgolfier balloon lifted the Marquis d'Arlandes and Jean-François Pilâtre de Rozier. They rose from the center of Paris.

The following month, French physicist Jacques Alexandre Cesar Charles filled a rubberized silk balloon with lighter-than-air hydrogen gas and flew 27 miles (43 km) from Paris.

1860s Military balloons

Most of the early uses of balloons were in warfare, lifting engineers to see the enemy or to send signals. Both armies in the American Civil War (1861-1865) used observation balloons.

1852 Henry Giffard

1900 Zeppelin LZ1

Held together by aluminum frame

LZ1

1884 Renard and Krebs

1919 R34

R34

R 34

1916 Caquot

Rigid frame

Stabilizing fin

Balloons float with the wind, but pilots of powered airships choose their course. Frenchman Henri Giffard built the first. Its steam engine propelled it forward at 6 mph (10 km/h). In 1852 he flew it from Paris to Trappes.

The first airship to complete a circular course was La France, a silk and bamboo airship made by Frenchmen Charles Renard and Arthur C. Krebs. It was equipped with an electric motor that drove it at 14.5 mph (23 km/h).

German Ferdinand Graf von Zeppelin perfected the airship. His first craft was a 420-ft (130-m) long LZ1. Later, larger "zeppelins" ferried 24 passengers between Germany and South America at 68 mph (100 km/h).

Military balloonists had to experiment with shapes to find the most stable balloon possible. One very effective type was the French-designed Caquot. It withstood gale-force winds, and rose to 6,000 ft (1,800 m).

During World War I (1914-1918), German forces dropped bombs on Britain from zeppelins. The British shot several down, and later copied their design for the peacetime R-34. In 1919 it flew a round-trip to NY State.

1936 Explorer II

1936 Hindenberg

Tail fin

1990s Skyship 500

G-BIHN

1980-90s Hot-air balloon

1978 Double Eagle II

Control/passenger gondola

The German zeppelin Hindenberg launched the first scheduled transatlantic passenger flight in 1936, crossing in as little as 52 hours. But in its first season of service, the craft's hydrogen filling caught fire, killing 35 people.

Swiss Auguste Piccard set the world high-altitude balloon record at 53,133 ft (16,201 m) in 1932, traveling in his balloon *Explorer II*. This had a spherical gondola (cabin). Later, Piccard designed a bathyscaphe to explore the ocean depths.

By far the most numerous lighter-than-air flying machines are hot-air balloons like the ones designed by the Montgolfier brothers in France. Modern hot-air balloons are made from nylon and filled with hot air from a gas burner.

Crossing the Atlantic in a balloon had been a balloonist's dream since the first attempt in 1873. A little more than a century later in 1978, Americans Ben Abruzzo, Maxie Anderson, and Larry Newman succeeded in their helium balloon Double Eagle II.

Modern airships, like the Skyship 500 are filled with nonflammable helium and built from lightweight composite materials. Their slow airspeed and long flying times make them useful for advertising, scientific work, and prospecting.

HELICOPTERS AND AUTOGYROS

15th century Leonardo

Leonardo's design, called an "airscrew"

1923 Cierva autogyro

Free-spinning blades

Rudder

Aircraft engine

1907-8 Paul Cornu

1940 Focke-Achgelis Fa 223

Tail fin like an airplane

Open cockpit

1939 Sikorsky VS-300

Italian artist and engineer Leonardo da Vinci (1452-1519) sketched the first helicopter in 1483. His craft was far ahead of technology then, but could not have flown.

French aviator Paul Cornu built the first working helicopter in 1907-8. Powered by a 24-hp (18 kW) engine, it could lift two passengers about 5 ft (1.5 m) up into the air.

Spanish engineer Juan de la Cierva replaced airplane wings with a rotor and called it an autogyro. Unlike a helicopter, the rotor only provides lift – the propeller actually moves the craft.

Germany's Focke-Wulf Company was the first to build a really practical helicopter in 1936. It could only lift the pilot, but by 1940, the Fa 223 could also carry passengers.

Igor Sikorsky (1889-1972) left his native Russia after the Russian Revolution and started to design and build helicopters in the US. Modern single-rotor helicopters are based on his VS-300.

1942 Sikorsky XR-4

Glass-enclosed cockpit

Tail wheel

1962 Sikorsky Skycrane

1965 Bell AH-1 HueyCobra

Slim fuselage

Minimal cockpit turns helicopter into flying crane.

1945 Bell model 47

Lightweight tail frame

"Goldfish bowl" cockpit gave all-around view.

1959 Sikorsky Sea King

The helicopter developed from a clumsy novelty into a useful aircraft in 1942, when Sikorsky built the XR4 and prototype two-seater helicopters. More than 130 of these were built for the US Army and Air Force.

The American Bell Aircraft corporation created a classic with its model 47. Its "goldfish bowl" cockpit gave a pilot and two passengers an all-around view. Bell built thousands of the model 47 for air forces in over 30 countries.

A hovering helicopter makes an easy target. Bell built their AH-1 HueyCobra helicopter with a specially slim fuselage less than 3 ft (1 m) wide so that it would be a much more difficult target to hit.

The Sea King, familiar from lifesaving air-sea rescue missions, was first built to hunt submarines. A sub-detecting probe was lowered from the Sea King. The crew launched torpedoes on any subs the probe spotted.

A helicopter with a crane can reach areas far from roads. The Sikorsky Skycrane, which first flew in 1962, was designed for military transportation, but many civilian versions are also in use, particularly in the oil industry.

1984 Hughes Apache

1959 Boeing Vertol 114 Chinook

1966 Bell Jetranger

1974 Aérospatiale Super Puma

1974 UH-60 Black Hawk

Like some of the earliest helicopters, the Boeing Chinook (or CH-47A) has twin horizontal rotors. Two powerful engines give the Chinook enormous lifting capacity: it can carry more than 40 equipped soldiers, or two tons of cargo.

Sweeping high above the Miami coastline, a Bell Jetranger leads the US government's war against drugs. The four-seater light helicopter was introduced in 1966, and was an instant success: Bell built 5,000 of the craft over the next 15 years.

Many helicopters are built in both civilian and military versions. Aérospatiale's Super Puma civilian helicopter carries diplomats and business people, while the military version, the Cougar, can carry 29 crack French army commandos into action.

As the main battlefield helicopter for the US Army, the Black Hawk is perhaps the safest helicopter ever built. It was designed to withstand a direct hit from antiaircraft guns, and in 1983, a Black Hawk landed safely after being hit a total of 48 times.

The menacing outline of the Apache attack helicopter strikes fear into its foes. Laden with the latest weaponry, it is a dangerous sight. The helicopter carries armor and other defensive features to help the crew survive a crash or attack.

Space

1232 First Chinese rockets

People nicknamed the first rockets "arrows of flying fire."

T he first rockets were little more than fireworks: the townspeople of Kai-feng-fu in China used them to propel arrows toward the Mongol soldiers who surrounded their town in AD 1232.

1900 War rockets

These rockets were launched from tubes, and a direct hit was fatal.

F or the next seven centuries, warfare and entertainment were almost the only uses for rockets. This ironclad weapon from 1900 had an explosive head and a range of about 325 yards (300 m).

1926 Robert H. Goddard

Goddard fueled his first rocket with gasoline and liquid oxygen.

M echanical genius Robert Goddard (1882-1945) was the first to launch a liquid-fueled rocket in 1926. By 1935, Goddard had perfected a stabilized rocket that flew as high as 7,500 ft (2,300 m).

1942 V-2

The V-2s often missed their targets or exploded in flight, but they were the prototypes for post-war rocket science.

W orld War II (1939-45) reawakened interest in rocket weapons. From a base at Peenemünde, German army engineers launched V-2 rockets against their enemies in London and Antwerp.

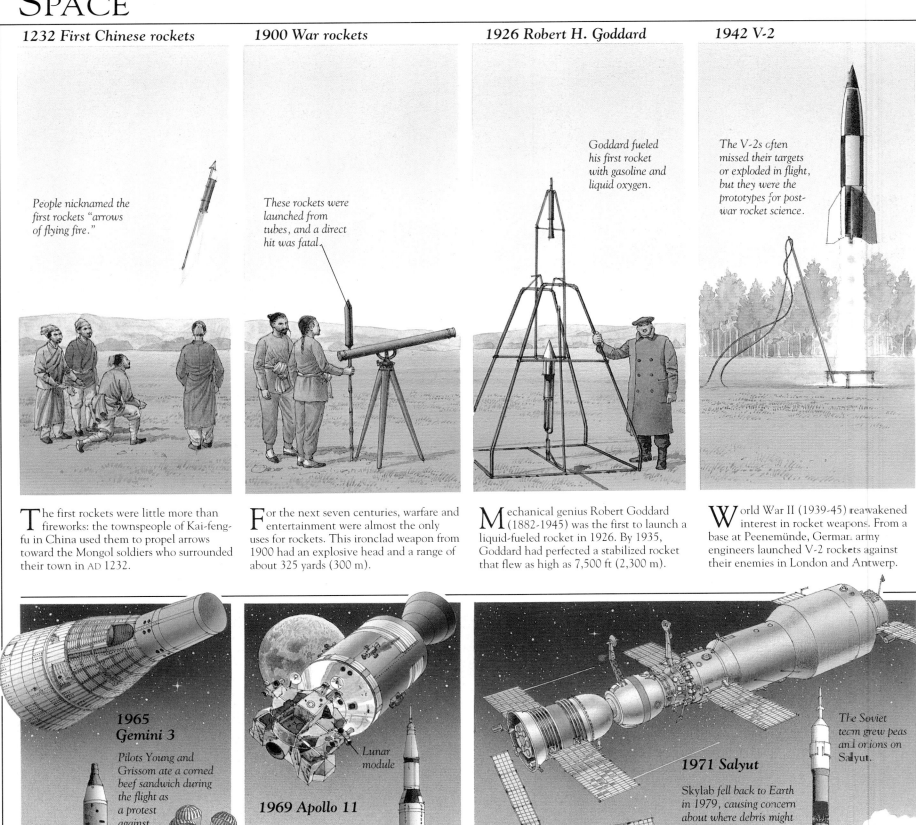

1965 Gemini 3

Pilots Young and Grissom ate a corned beef sandwich during the flight as a protest against their bland space diet.

Gemini 3 splashed down after three orbits.

1969 Apollo 11

Lunar module

Apollo 11 crew member Michael Collins (b. 1930) orbited the Moon in the command module that would ferry all three home.

1973 Skylab

Equipment left on Moon

1971 Salyut

The Soviet team grew peas and onions on Salyut.

Skylab fell back to Earth in 1979, causing concern about where debris might land – most landed in the Indian Ocean and Australian desert.

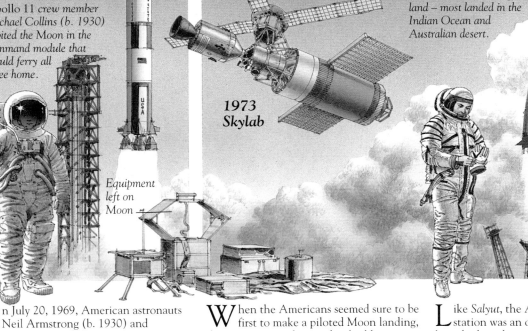

T he American Gemini program prepared astronauts for a mission to the Moon. It tested their ability to survive zero gravity (weightlessness) and helped develop methods for space capsules to meet up in space and lock together.

O n July 20, 1969, American astronauts Neil Armstrong (b. 1930) and "Buzz" Aldrin (b. 1930) stepped out of their landing vehicle and walked on the Moon. Instruments continued research after they departed.

W hen the Americans seemed sure to be first to make a piloted Moon landing, the Soviets turned instead to building space stations in Earth orbit. They launched the first, *Salyut 1*, and later ferried out a crew of 3 that stayed more than 3 weeks.

L ike *Salyut*, the American *Skylab* space station was an orbiting laboratory, launched on the massive *Saturn V* rocket. Both 3-man crews carried out experiments in zero gravity and used sophisticated on-board telescopes to photograph the Sun.

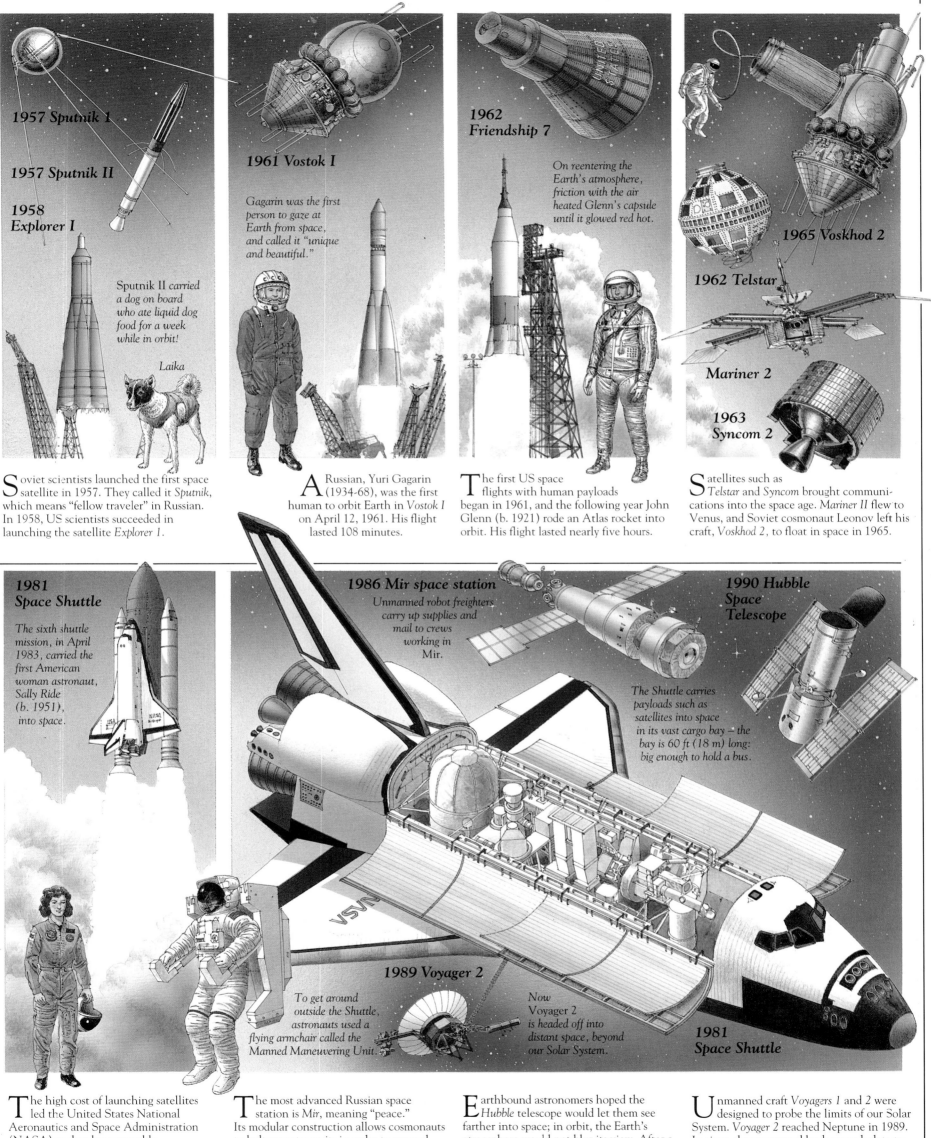

1957 Sputnik 1

1957 Sputnik II

1958 Explorer I

Sputnik II carried a dog on board who ate liquid dog food for a week while in orbit!

Laika

1961 Vostok I

Gagarin was the first person to gaze at Earth from space, and called it "unique and beautiful."

1962 Friendship 7

On reentering the Earth's atmosphere, friction with the air heated Glenn's capsule until it glowed red hot.

1965 Voskhod 2

1962 Telstar

Mariner 2

1963 Syncom 2

Soviet scientists launched the first space satellite in 1957. They called it *Sputnik*, which means "fellow traveler" in Russian. In 1958, US scientists succeeded in launching the satellite *Explorer 1*.

A Russian, Yuri Gagarin (1934-68), was the first human to orbit Earth in *Vostok I* on April 12, 1961. His flight lasted 108 minutes.

The first US space flights with human payloads began in 1961, and the following year John Glenn (b. 1921) rode an Atlas rocket into orbit. His flight lasted nearly five hours.

Satellites such as *Telstar* and *Syncom* brought communications into the space age. *Mariner II* flew to Venus, and Soviet cosmonaut Leonov left his craft, *Voskhod 2*, to float in space in 1965.

1981 Space Shuttle

The sixth shuttle mission, in April 1983, carried the first American woman astronaut, Sally Ride (b. 1951), into space.

1986 Mir space station

Unmanned robot freighters carry up supplies and mail to crews working in Mir.

1990 Hubble Space Telescope

The Shuttle carries payloads such as satellites into space in its vast cargo bay – the bay is 60 ft (18 m) long: big enough to hold a bus.

1989 Voyager 2

To get around outside the Shuttle, astronauts used a flying armchair called the Manned Maneuvering Unit.

Now Voyager 2 is headed off into distant space, beyond our Solar System.

1981 Space Shuttle

The high cost of launching satellites led the United States National Aeronautics and Space Administration (NASA) to develop a reusable launch vehicle, the Space Shuttle, in 1981.

The most advanced Russian space station is *Mir*, meaning "peace." Its modular construction allows cosmonauts to bolt on extra units in order to expand the station's functions. Crews on *Mir* have stayed in orbit longer than anyone.

Earthbound astronomers hoped the *Hubble* telescope would let them see farther into space; in orbit, the Earth's atmosphere would not blur its view. After a fault in the telescope's mirrors was repaired, it fulfilled its potential.

Unmanned craft *Voyagers 1* and 2 were designed to probe the limits of our Solar System. *Voyager 2* reached Neptune in 1989. In time, they may send back enough data to help us understand more about the origins of our universe – and the "Big Bang" theory.

BIOGRAPHICAL INDEX

THIS INDEX CONTAINS BRIEF BIOGRAPHIES of the inventors, innovators, engineers, architects, and scientists mentioned in the book. For other figures, such as politicians or (for example) pioneer pilots who did not design or build the aircraft they flew, see the general index.

ARISTOPHANES
(c.448 BC–c.388 BC) *Greek* p44
Playwright Aristophanes wrote the first description of the action of a lens.

ARKWRIGHT, RICHARD
(1732–92) *English* p48
Inventor and industrialist Richard Arkwright patented a spinning-frame to speed the production of yarn and installed the machine in one of Britain's first factories.

BAIRD, JOHN LOGIE
(1888–1946) *Scottish* p42
Electrical engineer John Logie Baird was the first to devise a television, but his version was rapidly replaced by an all-electronic television. A productive inventor all his life, he came up with many other ideas.

BELL, ALEXANDER GRAHAM
(1847–1922) *Scottish-American* p43
Alexander Graham Bell invented the telephone in Canada while investigating ways of teaching the deaf to speak. He built the first successful telephone in 1876, and was granted a patent the following year.

BENZ, KARL FRIEDRICH
(1844–1929) *German* p57
Karl Benz developed a reliable two-stroke gasoline engine in 1879. It was not a commercial success, and he based his famous 1885 car on a four-stroke engine.

BERLINER, EMILE
(1851–1929) *German-American* p44
Before emigrating to the US in 1870, Emile Berliner was a trainee printer in Germany. In the US he patented several improvements to the telephone, and was the first to record sound on flat disks, in 1888. His method of pressing disks survived essentially unchanged for nearly a century.

BESSEMER, HENRY
(1813–98) *English* p49
One of inventor and industrialist Henry Bessemer's most important contributions to metallurgy came when war increased the demand for steel. He made steel manufacture less expensive by blowing air through molten iron.

BIRO, LADISLAO
(1900–1985) *Hungarian* p40
Ladislao Biro made the first successful ballpoint pens.

BLANCHARD, THOMAS
(1788–1864) *American* p48
Blanchard's copying lathe, built in 1818, was one of the first machines that did not need skilled operators.

BLÉRIOT, LOUIS
(1872–1936) *French* p65
Blériot designed the first tractor monoplanes – single-winged aircraft pulled, rather than pushed, by a propeller.

BORDINO, VIRGILIO
(1804–1878) *Italian* p56
Bordino built a novel coal-driven steam carriage in 1854.

Bordino's steam carriage

BROUGHAM, HENRY
(1778–1868) *Scottish* p52
Brougham designed a horse-drawn carriage for his own use that became widely adopted for city transportation.

BRUNEL, ISAMBARD KINGDOM
(1806–59) *English* p62
Brunel worked on a vast range of civil engineering projects, but ships were perhaps his greatest achievement. Along with John Russell, he designed the *Great Eastern*. Launched in 1858, it remained the world's largest vessel for 40 years. It was a commercial failure, but became a cable-laying ship. Worry over the project hastened his death.

BRUNEL, MARC ISAMBARD
(1769–1849) *French-English* p49
Marc Brunel fled to America to escape the French Revolution. He became chief engineer for New York City, but in 1799 sailed for England, where he constructed the first tunnel under the Thames River.

BRUNELLESCHI, FILIPPO
(1377–1446) *Italian* p32
Filippo Brunelleschi trained as a goldsmith and sculptor. He worked in and around Florence and is best known for his dome, which tops the city's cathedral.

BURTON, DECIMUS
(1800–1881) *English* p32
Architect Decimus Burton designed a magnificent palm house at Kew Botanical Gardens and laid out London's Hyde Park.

CARLSON, CHESTER FLOYD
(1906–1968) *American* p41
Patent lawyer Chester Carlson sought a rapid copying method that used no film, camera, or wet chemicals. It took him six years to develop. He patented a dry copy system, but he did not find a company to make and market the invention until 1944.

CASELLI, GIOVANNI
(1815–1891) *Italian* p43
Caselli devised one of the first facsimile (fax) machines.

Modern fax machine

CAYLEY, GEORGE
(1773–1857) *English* p64
Gentleman inventor George Cayley was among the first to build practical gliders. Though he aimed to build powered aircraft, he recognized that this would be possible only when lighter, more powerful engines were available.

CHAPPE, CLAUDE
(1763–1805) *French* p43
Claude Chappe devised an optical method of transmitting messages in 1790. He devoted his life to building a vast network of telegraph stations.

CIERVA, JUAN DE LA
(1895–1936) *Spanish* p67
Engineer Juan de la Cierva invented the autogyro – a propeller-driven aircraft lifted by a freewheeling rotor.

CLYMER, GEORGE
(1754–1834) *American* p40
Clymer built the first iron printing press in the US in 1813. It was also the first to work without a screw.

COLT, SAMUEL
(1814–1862) *American* p29
Colt made the revolver a reliable weapon. He was 21 when he patented the famous six-shooter. A business genius as well as a skilled engineer, he eventually became very rich.

Outlaws favored Colt revolvers

CORBUSIER *see* JEANNERET

CORNU, PAUL
(1881–1944) *French* p67
Paul Cornu was the first to build a working helicopter.

CRAMPTON, THOMAS RUSSELL
(1816–1888) *English* p58
Engineer Thomas Crampton designed some of the fastest steam locomotives of the mid-19th century.

CRICK, FRANCIS HARRY COMPTON
(1916–) *English* p26
In 1953, working with James Watson and Maurice Wilkins, molecular biologist Francis Crick built a model of DNA – the "genetic code" molecule that controls the growth and development of all living things. The three men were awarded the Nobel Prize in 1962.

CUGNOT, NICOLAS JOSEPH
(1725–1804) *French* p56
Artillery officer Nicolas Cugnot built one of the first self-propelled road vehicles. It was powered by a steam engine.

CURIE, MARIE
(1867–1934) *Polish-French* p27
Physicist Marie Curie found the element radium and discovered the nature of radioactivity. She was the first woman to win the Nobel Prize, sharing it with her husband Pierre, and Henri Becquerel. Exposure to radiation eventually killed her.

CURIE, PIERRE
(1859–1906) *Polish-French* p27
Chemist Pierre Curie studied radioactivity and magnetism with his wife Marie. Together with Henri Becquerel, he developed an electrometer (electric charge meter), which proved vital in their research.

CURTISS, GLENN HAMMOND
(1878–1930) *American* p65
Curtiss added an engine to a balloon and then constructed heavier-than-air craft. He built the first practical seaplane, but his most lasting feat was the development of the aileron control surface that all modern aircraft use in turning.

DA VINCI *see* VINCI

DAGUERRE, LOUIS JACQUES MANDÉ
(1787–1851) *French* p45
Daguerre carried out early photographic research with Nicéphore Niépce. But the daguerreotype photographs that he unveiled six years after Niepce's death used a totally different process

DAIMLER, GOTTLIEB
(1834–1900) *German* p55
Engineer Gottlieb Daimler built the first high-speed internal combustion engine. He also devised a carburetor, which allowed his motors to run on liquid fuels. He used the engines to power the first motorcycle and an early car.

Daimler's motorcycle

DARBY, ABRAHAM I
(c.1678–1717) *English* p46, 48
Ironmaster Abraham Darby I was the first to use coke to fuel iron-smelting furnaces. This breakthrough greatly increased Britain's output of cast iron.

DARBY, ABRAHAM III
(1750–91) *English* p36
Ironworker Abraham Darby III perfected the use of cast iron, building a spectacular bridge across the Severn River.

DICKSON, WILLIAM KENNEDY LAURIE
(1860–1935) *English-French* p44
While employed by Thomas Edison, optical engineer William Dickson is thought to have built most of the Kinetoscope movie system that Edison claimed as his own.

DRAIS, KARL VON
(1785–1851) *German* p54
In 1817, Karl von Drais built a cycle with a steerable front wheel that was the forerunner of the bicycle.

DRAKE, EDWIN L.
(1819–1880) *American* p47
Edwin Drake drilled the first oil well in the United States at Titusville, Pennsylvania in 1859.

EDISON, THOMAS ALVA
(1847–1931) *American* p45
Thomas Edison patented his first invention at 21 – the ticker tape machine that broadcast stock exchange data. He is most famous for inventing sound recording, the light-bulb, and movies. He built the first research laboratory, and thus invented a new way of inventing.

EHRLICH, PAUL
(1854–1915) *German* p27
Bacteriologist Paul Ehrlich was the first to propose that a drug could be a "magic bullet," seeking out an organism causing disease. He found a cure for the then-fatal sexually transmitted disease syphilis. He shared a Nobel Prize in 1908.

EILMER
(980-1066) *English p64*
The bone-breaking jump of Monk Eilmer, also known as Oliver of Malmesbury, is one of the first documented attempts at human flight.

EVANS, OLIVER
(1755-1819) *American p49*
Evans designed an automatic flour mill in 1785 that had advanced labor-saving mechanisms to speed production.

FERMI, ENRICO
(1901-1954) *Italian-American p46*
Nuclear physicist Enrico Fermi was part of an Italian team that produced the first artificial radioactive substances in 1934. In 1938 he won a Nobel Prize, but fled to the US to escape Italy's fascist government. There, Fermi built the first nuclear reactor and worked on the atomic bomb.

FERRARI, ENZO
(1898-1988) *Italian p56*
Race car driver Ferrari founded the Ferrari motor company in 1929 and began designing cars 11 years later.

FLEMING, ALEXANDER
(1881-1955) *Scottish p26*
Bacteriologist Alexander Fleming is best known for his discovery of the first antibiotic drug. He was also the first to use a vaccine against typhoid.

FORD, HENRY
(1863-1947) *American p48*
Carmaker Henry Ford produced a gasoline-driven car in 1896 and started the Ford Motor Company in 1903. Ford's radical ideas about mass-production turned the car from a hand-built luxury into affordable transportation.

FOX TALBOT *see* TALBOT

FRANKLIN, BENJAMIN
(1706-90) *American p66*
Scientist and statesman Benjamin Franklin carried out important electrical experiments and was responsible for many innovations and inventions, including the lightning conductor and bifocal spectacles. As a politician, he is most famous for his role in engineering America's independence from Britain.

FRANKLIN, ROSALIND ELSIE
(1920-1958) *English p26*
Biophysicist Rosalind Franklin used X-ray diffraction to study the DNA molecule. Her work helped the Nobel Prize-winning team to find the molecule's spiral structure, but her contribution has only recently been recognized.

FREUD, SIGMUND
(1856-1939) *Austrian p27*
Sigmund Freud pioneered the treatment of mental illness by analysis – drawing out buried thoughts through conversations with patients. Disputed at the time, his ideas are now widely accepted.

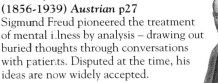

GALILEI, GALILEO
(1564-1642) *Italian p45*
One of the greatest scientific geniuses the world has ever known, Galileo Galilei was responsible for many discoveries. From 1609 Galileo used the telescope to study astronomy, and in 1633 he was imprisoned for supporting the idea that the Earth orbits the Sun.

GALILEO *see* GALILEI

GIBBON, JOHN HEYNSHAM
(1903-73) *American p26*
John Gibbon invented the heart-lung machine that made open-heart surgery possible.

GIFFARD, HENRI
(1825-1882) *French p66*
Henri Giffard flew the first airship (powered balloon).

GILBRETH, FRANK
(1868-1924) *American p48*
In partnership with his wife, Lillian, engineer Frank Gilbreth helped introduce ideas about time-and-motion study and scientific management to American industry.

GILBRETH, LILLIAN
(1878-1972) *American p48*
Psychologist Lillian Gilbreth was a pioneer of time-and-motion study and scientific management. With her husband, Frank, she ran a management consultancy.

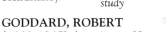

Time-and-motion study

GODDARD, ROBERT
(1882-1945) *American p68*
Goddard invented the liquid-fueled rocket. He devised ways of controlling his craft by jet vanes and gyroscopes.

GRAMME, ZENOBE THÉOPHILE
(1826-1901) *Belgian p46*
Gramme developed an efficient generator in 1873. Its high output helped make electric power popular.

GRESLEY, (HERBERT) NIGEL
(1876-1941) *Scottish p58, 59*
Gresley was Britain's last great steam locomotive designer.

GUTENBERG, JOHANNES GENSFLEISCH
(c.1398-1468) *German p40*
Gutenberg often takes the credit for the "invention" of printing with movable type. It would be fairer to say that he was among the first Europeans to exploit the technology for profit. His work helped spread printing worldwide.

HIPPOCRATES
(c.460-377 BC) *Greek p27*
Physician Hippocrates is best known for the oath named after him, with which even today's doctors swear to serve humanity. He probably did not write the oath. Perhaps his most important idea was that doctors should observe and experiment to diagnose illness.

HOHENHEIM, THEOPHRASTUS BOMBASTUS VON (1493-1541)
German-Swiss p26
Using the pseudonym *Paracelsus*, his controversial views made him many enemies, but he was responsible for some important medical principles that we now take for granted.

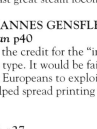

JACQUARD, JOSEPH MARIE
(1752-1834) *French p48*
Jacquard built the first automatic loom capable of weaving patterned fabrics in 1801. His use of punched cards to encode the patterns was revolutionary.

JANSSEN, HANS & ZACHARIAS
Dutch p45
Spectacle-makers Zacharias Janssen and his father, Hans, built the first multiple lens microscope around 1590.

JEANNERET, CHARLES
(1887-1965) *Swiss-French p23*
Better known as *Le Corbusier,* Jeanneret was perhaps the 20th century's most influential architect. He thought of buildings as "machines for living," and designed them in a distinctive, blocklike style with little decoration.

JENNER, EDWARD
(1749-1823) *English p27*
Jenner was the first to study vaccination in a scientific way. He published his discoveries in 1796, and though there was strong opposition at first, vaccination was soon widely accepted as protection against smallpox.

JENNEY, WILLIAM LE BARON
(1832-1907) *American p32*
Jenney was one of the first skyscraper designers, using a strong metal frame to support his structures.

JOHNSON, DENNIS
English p54
Dennis Johnson patented a prototype bicycle in 1818.

KNOLL, MAX
(1897-1969) *German p45*
Knoll was involved in the development of the world's first electron microscope and scanning electron microscope.

Scanning electron microscope

KÖNIG, FREDERICK
(1774-1833) *German p41*
German Frederick König built the first steam-powered printing press in 1810. The London newspaper *The Times* was printed on a powered press in 1814.

KÜHNHOLD, RUDOLPH
(1903-) *German p45*
Chief of the German Navy's Signals Research department Rudolph Kühnhold demonstrated a crude but working radar system in Kiel in 1934.

LALLEMENT, PIERRE
(b.1843) *French p54*
Lallement replaced crank (to-and-fro) bicycle pedals with today's rotary variety.

LAND, EDWIN
(1909-1991) *American p44*
Scientist and industrialist Edwin Land became interested in polarized light while a student at Harvard University. In 1932, he demonstrated a method of making the antiglare polarizing material now used in sunglasses and photographic filters. But his greatest success came in 1947 when he invented instant photography.

LE CORBUSIER *see* JEANNERET

LEEUWENHOEK, ANTON VAN
(1632-1723) *Dutch p45*
Merchant Anton van Leeuwenhoek started building microscopes as a hobby. His tiny instruments used one simple lens, but worked better than the compound (multi-lens) microscopes of the time. Magnifying his subjects 200 times, he was the first to see, draw, and describe bacteria, red blood cells, and sperm.

LILIENTHAL, OTTO
(1848-1896) *German p64*
Fascinated by flight even as a boy, aeronaut Otto Lilienthal began experiments with gliders in 1881. Though most of his craft were hang gliders, he also built a flapping-wing flying machine powered by a small engine. He was killed when one his gliders crashed.

LIND, JAMES
(1716-1794) *Scottish p27*
Lind discovered that lime juice cured the vitamin C deficiency scurvy, which until the mid-18th century had killed thousands of sailors. He studied medicine only after serving as a surgeon's mate on a naval ship. On graduation, he worked in a naval hospital. Though he published his cure in 1753, it took the British navy 40 years to adopt it.

LIPPERSHEY, HANS
(c.1570-c.1619) *Dutch p45*
Spectacle-maker Hans Lippershey probably invented the telescope. According to Dutch tradition, he looked through two aligned lenses, and noticed that a distant object appeared enlarged. He applied for a patent on the telescope in 1608. The use of telescopes spread rapidly throughout Europe during the seventeenth century.

LISTER, JOSEPH
(1827-1912) *English p26*
Surgeon Joseph Lister did his pioneering research on reducing infection while working in Scotland. Lister's antiseptic methods revolutionized surgery and the survival rate of patients increased. Despite this, his techniques were not accepted by doctors when he first published them. Lister operated on the English queen Victoria and carried out important work on blood clotting. He was knighted for his services to medicine.

LUN, TSAI
(c.50-118) *Chinese p41*
Chinese tradition credits court official Tsai Lun with the invention of paper around AD 105. In western Europe, paper began to be used in the 15th century.

BIOGRAPHICAL INDEX

MACMILLAN, KIRKPATRICK
(1813-1878) *Scottish* p54
Scottish blacksmith Macmillan
built one of the first bicycles
around 1839. The
design remained almost
unchanged for 20 years.

Macmillan's bicycle

MAILLART, ROBERT
(1872-1940) *Swiss* p37
Maillart built some of the first reinforced-concrete bridges
in which a roadway and its supports form a single unit.
Examples such as Salginatobel, which span deep mountain
valleys, are graceful yet amazing engineering feats.

MARCONI, GUGLIELMO
(1874-1937) *Italian* p42
Physics student Guglielmo Marconi began experiments
with radio at the age of 20. Within a year he had sent
messages more than a mile. He moved to England to
perfect and patent his invention, and in 1901 he sent
the first radio messages across the Atlantic. He shared
the Nobel Prize for physics in 1909. On his death, radio
stations worldwide honored him by broadcasting two
minutes of silence.

MAUDSLAY, HENRY
(1771-1831) *English* p49
Engineer Henry Maudslay was the inventor of one of the
first precision lathes made of metal. He realized that the
future of engineering depended on precise measurement,
and built a micrometer capable of measuring distances as
small as 1/10,000 of an inch. He worked with Marc Brunel
(see above) to create the world's first mass-production
machinery. The machines were used to make blocks
(pulleys) for Britain's Royal Navy.

MAXIM, HIRAM S.
(1840-1916) *American-English* p28
Maxim invented a flying
machine, an electric light, and
smokeless gunpowder. He
invented a better mousetrap, too.
However, the world beat a path
to his door not for the Maxim
mousetrap, but for the
Maxim machine gun.

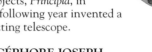
Maxim machine gun

MAYBACH, WILHELM
(1847-1929) *German* p55
In cooperation with Gottlieb Daimler, engineer Wilhelm
Maybach built a gasoline-engine motorcycle.

MIES VAN DER ROHE, LUDWIG
(1886-1969) *German-American* p33
Pioneering designer of glass-faced skyscrapers Mies van der
Rohe began his career in Germany. In the 1930s the rise of
Nazism drove him to the US. His most famous work there
is the Seagram building in New York City.

MONTGOLFIER, JACQUES ÉTIENNE
(1745-1799) *French* p66
Montgolfier and his brother Joseph made the first hot-air
balloon in 1783, as well as a passenger-carrying balloon.

MONTGOLFIER, JOSEPH MICHEL
(1740-1810) *French* p66 *See above*

MORSE, SAMUEL FINLEY BREESE
(1791-1872) *American* p43
Morse devised an electric telegraph when studying
chemistry and electricity in 1832. He demonstrated a
working system to the US Congress five years later. His
idea brought him wealth only after the first telegraph line
opened in 1844, between Washington D.C. and
Baltimore, Maryland.

MORTON, WILLIAM (1819-1868)
American p26
Dentist William Morton pioneered the
use of ether to make patients
unconscious during surgery.

MOULTON, ALEXANDER
(1920-) *English* p54
Alex Moulton designed the
first successful small-wheel
bicycle around 1957.

Moulton bicycle

NASMYTH, JAMES
(1808-1890) *Scottish* p49
As a child, engineer James Nasmyth made such superb
model engines that he was asked to build a full-size steam
carriage. His steam hammer of 1839 made possible the
accurate forging of huge metal parts.

NEWCOMEN, THOMAS
(1663-1729) *English* p47
Newcomen was the first to use steam power to pump water
automatically. The machine infringed on an earlier patent
by Thomas Savery, forcing Newcomen to make Savery a
partner. Despite its huge appetite for coal, the Newcomen
pump was a great success, but Newcomen probably saw
little of the profit.

NEWTON, ISAAC
(1642-1727) *English* p44
Scientist and mathematician Isaac
Newton was 23 when the sight of a
falling apple gave him ideas about
gravity. His later writings on science
and mathematics were works of
genius, and few would deny that
Newton was one of the greatest
scientists of all time. He published
his most important work on gravity
and moving objects, *Principia*, in
1687, and the following year invented a
practical reflecting telescope.

NIÉPCE, NICÉPHORE JOSEPH
(1765-1833) *French* p45
Niépce experimented with cameras from 1816 on. He
caught an image from a lens on sensitized paper that year,
but it took another six years before he could fix pictures
permanently.

OLDS, RANSOM E.
(1864-1950) *American* p56
Olds was the first to produce cars in significant numbers.
By the time he left *Oldsmobile* in 1904, the company had
made 4,000 Curved-dash Runabouts.

PANHARD, RENÉ
(1841-1908) *French* p57
In partnership with Émile Levassor, René Panhard built
some early cars that set important standards for the layout
of components and controls.

PARACELSUS *see* **HOHENHEIM**

PARSONS, CHARLES
(1854-1931) *Irish-English* p63
Parsons joined an electrical engineering firm after college
and developed his first steam turbines to power the
company's generators. After making record-breaking
turbine-powered marine engines, Parsons turned to
building large telescopes, as did his father (see below).

PARSONS, WILLIAM
(1800-1867) *Irish* p44
Parsons carried out important early research into the
construction of large reflecting telescope mirrors.

PASTEUR, LOUIS
(1822-1895) *French* p26
Pasteur's studies of fermentation led
to the preservation of foods by heat-
treatment, an achievement for which
the scientist still receives credit
on every milk carton. Pasteur's
important discoveries in the field
of immunization made possible
modern shots that protect against
diseases, including previously fatal
diseases such as rabies.

PICCARD, AUGUSTE ANTOINE
(1884-1962) *Swiss* p66
Piccard explored both the high atmosphere and the ocean
depths. On his 1930s balloon flights, he was the first man
into the stratosphere. Told that the construction of a
spherical gondola for a balloon was impossible, he ordered
a spherical beer barrel instead, which he promptly
converted into the required gondola. In 1953 he descended
10,330 ft (3,150 m) below the surface of the ocean in a
bathyscaphe craft of his own design.

PITMAN, ISAAC
(1813-1897) *English* p40
Pitman published the shorthand
system that made him famous
when he was 24. Pitman
shorthand recorded the sounds
of speech, rather than spelling
the words letter by letter. It is
still widely used to write down words
as fast as almost anyone can say them.

POLLIO, MARCUS VITRUVIUS
(FL.46-30 BC) *Roman* p46
Engineer Marcus Pollio Vitruvius wrote the only Roman
work on architecture that has survived to the present day.

POULSEN, VALDEMAR
(1869-1942) *Danish* p44
Poulsen devised a way of recording sound magnetically on
a reel of steel wire. His Telegraphone was the forerunner of
the tape recorder.

PRINCE, LOUIS AIMÉ AUGUSTIN LE
(1842-1890) *French* p44
Louis Le Prince was the first to demonstrate a method of
making movies, but he mysteriously disappeared before he
could develop a commercial camera and projector.

REBER, GROTE
(1911-) *American* p44
Radio engineer Grote Reber built the first radio telescope.

RENARD, CHARLES
(1847-1905) *French* p66
Engineer Charles Renard built one of the first airships.

ROE, EDWIN ALLIOT VERDON
(1877-1958) *English* p65
Engineer A.V. Roe built and flew the first British
airplanes. His AVRO company later manufactured military
aircraft in large numbers.

AVRO 504 biplane

ROEBLING, JOHN
(1806-1869) *German-American* p37
Engineer John Roebling emigrated to the United States at
age 25, but could not settle as a farmer, and turned to
making steel ropes. With these, he constructed a
magnificent suspension bridge across Niagara Falls. He
died during the construction of his masterpiece, New York
City's Brooklyn Bridge. His son, Washington, completed
the commission.

ROENTGEN *see* **RÖNTGEN**

ROHE, MIES VAN DER *see* **MIES**

RÖNTGEN, WILHELM CONRAD
(1845-1923) *German* p27
While a student of mechanical engineering, Wilhelm
Röntgen discovered that he was more interested in physics.
His change of career was a success – he became one of the
most brilliant experimental physicists of his time. His
greatest achievement was the discovery of X rays, for
which he received the first Nobel Prize for physics in 1901.

RUSKA, ERNST AUGUST FRIEDRICH
(1906-1988) *German* p45
Ruska built the first magnetic lens and, with Max Knoll,
invented the electron microscope. He shared the Nobel
Prize for physics in 1986.

SENEFELDER, ALOIS
(1771-1834) *German* p41
Enterprising actor and playwright Alois
Senefelder was seeking a quick and
inexpensive way of printing music
and scripts when he developed
lithography around 1796. After
perfecting the process, he opened a
Munich printing works in 1806 and
eventually became the director of
Germany's Royal Printing Office.

SHIH, TUAN CHENG
(born c.AD 800) *Chinese p44*
Shih described the principle of the camera obscura around AD 840. It was the forerunner of the photographic camera.

SHOLES, CHRISTOPHER
(1819-1890) *American p41*
Printer, journalist, and inventor Christopher Sholes built the first successful typewriter in 1874.

SICARD, ABBÉ
(1742-1822) *French p42*
Sicard developed one of the first practical sign languages, writing a book of French words and their sign equivalents.

SIKORSKY, IGOR IVANOVICH
(1889-1972) *Russian-American p67*
Sikorsky experimented with helicopters in 1910 in his native Russia, but none flew. He completed a successful helicopter in 1939 in the US. His VS-300 craft was the first to fly with a small tail rotor for stability.

Sikorsky VS-300

SPRECKELSEN, JOHAN OTTO VON
(1929-1987) *Danish p33*
Architect Johan Otto von Spreckelsen designed the Grand Arch that houses the French defense ministry in Paris.

STANLEY BROTHERS, F.E. AND F.O.
(F.E. 1849-1918 F.O. 1849-1940) *American p56*
At the start of the 20th century, the Stanley brothers developed steam-driven cars that briefly rivaled cars powered by internal combustion engines.

STARLEY, JAMES
(1831-1881) *English p55*
James Starley developed one of the first "penny-farthing" bicycles and the first bicycle wheels with wire spokes.

STARLEY, JOHN KEMP
(1854-1901) *English p54*
John Starley (nephew of James) built the "Rover" bicycle in 1886. Bicycles still follow his basic design.

STEPHENSON, GEORGE
(1781-1848) *English p58*
Stephenson taught himself to read and moved from stoking steam engines to building them. His locomotive Rocket hauled the world's first passenger train. He went on to oversee the expansion of the English railroad network.

STEPHENSON, ROBERT
(1803-59) *English p58*
Engineer Robert Stephenson began his career in the office of his father, George (see above), but later became famous for his bridges, rather than the locomotives that crossed them. The locomotive building company he founded made engines for many railroads.

Stephenson's Rocket

STROWGER, ALMON BROWN
(1839-1902) *American p43*
Annoyed with the telephone exhange operator giving business to a rival, undertaker Almon Strowger devised dial telephones and automatic exchanges that connected calls without a human operator.

TALBOT, WILLIAM HENRY FOX
(1800-1877) *English p45*
Physicist William Henry Fox Talbot invented his calotype photographic process in 1835. He announced it four years later when he learned that Louis Daguerre had independently invented a similar process in France. Talbot went on to produce the first book illustrated with photographs (1844-6).

THIMONNIER, BARTHÉLEMY
(1793-1859) *French p48*
Thimonnier invented one of the first sewing machines, but it was not a commercial success. The sewing machine was one of the first labor-saving devices to be used in the home.

Early sewing machine

TREVITHICK, RICHARD
(1771-1833) *English p58*
Trevithick constructed the first high-pressure stationary steam engines and, in 1804, the first railroad locomotive.

TURNER, RICHARD
(c.1798-1881) *Irish p32*
Turner provided architect Decimus Burton with the engineering expertise he needed to build his glass Palm House at the Royal Botanic Gardens in Kew, London.

UTZON, JØRN
(1918-) *Danish p33*
Architect Jørn Utzon won the competition held to find a design for Sydney's waterfront opera house.

VAIL, ALFRED
(1807-1859) *American p43*
Vail worked on Samuel Morse's electric telegraph, adding the operator's key and many other innovations without which the Morse telegraph could not have succeeded.

VAN DER ROHE *see* MIES

VAUBAN, SEBASTIEN LE PRESTRE DE
(1633-1707) *French p35*
Military engineer Sebastien de Vauban directed sieges for the French king, Louis XIV. Besides building massive, spectacular star-shaped forts, Vauban invented the socket bayonet and designed many other engineering structures.

VESALIUS, ANDREAS
(1514-1564) *Belgian p26*
To study anatomy, physician Andreas Vesalius bravely dissected corpses at a time when it was illegal. He was condemned to death for the crime, but eventually let off with the lighter sentence of having to make a pilgrimage (holy journey) to Jerusalem. He died on the return trip.

VINCI, LEONARDO DA
(1452-1519) *Italian p56, 67*
Famous as creator of the Mona Lisa (1504) and other paintings, da Vinci was also an engineer and inventor. Some of his engineering work was practical – in 1506 he was employed in building canals. However, it is a series of sketchbooks that demonstrate Leonardo's inventive genius. He filled the books with mechanical projects and studies of the natural world. Many of the inventions depicted, such as the helicopter, the tank, and the flying machine, did not become realities until the 20th century.

VITRUVIUS *see* POLLIO

VOISIN, CHARLES
(1882-1912) *French p65*
With his brother Gabriel, Voisin built some of France's first aircraft.

VOISIN, GABRIEL
(1880-1973) *French p65 See above*

VON DRAIS *see* DRAIS

WATERMAN, LEWIS EDSON
(1837-1901) *American p40*
Insurance salesman Lewis Waterman created the first fountain pen with a built-in ink supply after a blot from a conventional pen spoiled a policy, losing him a customer. Fountain pens developed into both lever-filling and squeeze-filling types. Ink cartridges came later.

WATSON, JAMES D.
(1928-) *American p26*
Biologist James Watson shared with Francis Crick and Maurice Wilkins a 1962 Nobel Prize for discovering the spiral structure of the DNA molecule, the basic building block of animal and plant life.

WATSON-WATT, ROBERT ALEXANDER
(1892-1973) *British p45*
A descendant of James Watt (see below), Watson-Watt led a team of British scientists that developed a practical radar system during World War II. This "secret weapon" helped Britain detect and destroy German bombers as they approached across the English Channel.

WATT, JAMES
(1736-1819) *Scottish p41*
While repairing a model of a Newcomen pumping engine (p47) Watt hit upon ways of cutting its fuel needs, thus improving Newcomen's design. In 1781 he built the first steam engine that turned wheels rather than pumped water. Many engines built by the firm he founded with Matthew Boulton worked until the late 1800s.

WILKINS, MAURICE HUGH FREDERICK
(1916-) *British-New Zealand p26*
Wilkins worked to discover the structure of DNA with Francis Crick and James Watson, sharing with them a Nobel Prize. His X rays of the genetic molecule showed that it was layered, and had a spiral shape.

WREN, CHRISTOPHER
(1632-1723) *English p32*
Wren is best known as the architect of London's St. Paul's Cathedral and many smaller churches in the city. When fire consumed much of London in 1666, Wren drafted an ambitious, and eventually unsuccessful, plan for the rebuilding of the whole city.

WRIGHT, ORVILLE
(1871-1948) *American p64*
Like his brother Wilbur (see below), Orville Wright was a bicycle mechanic by trade. But in control of the *Flyer* they built together, he became the first pilot of a powered aircraft in 1903.

WRIGHT, WILBUR
(1867-1912) *American p64*
Cycle engineer and flying pioneer Wilbur Wright constructed the first powered heavier-than-air flying machine with his brother Orville and mechanic Charles Taylor. Wilbur devised a wing-warping mechanism that enabled the brothers to control and turn their craft.

Flyer, 1903

WRIGHT, FRANK LLOYD
(1867-1959) *American p22*
Frank Lloyd Wright earned his reputation as a great architect largely through designs for private homes. However, his training as a civil engineer helped him use modern building methods and materials in extraordinary larger structures. Best known is New York City's Guggenheim Museum. Its floor slants continuously up, like a giant corkscrew.

ZEPPELIN, COUNT FERDINAND VON
(1838-1917) *German p66*
German army officer Ferdinand von Zeppelin invented the rigid airship at the end of the 19th century. He built military and civilian versions, but his experiments ended when his airship *Hindenberg* exploded at its mooring in New Jersey in 1937.

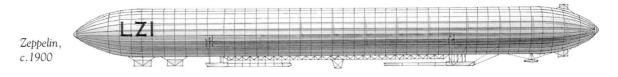
Zeppelin, c.1900

INDEX

ACKNOWLEDGMENTS
Dorling Kindersley would like to thank the following people who helped with this book:
Lynn Bresler for the index
Janet Abbott for additional research
Ford Motor Company Limited